Will
the Real Church
Please Stand!

A Conversion Journey
from Fundamental Baptist
to Roman Catholic

Anne Stokes

En Route Books and Media, LLC
Saint Louis, MO

Make the time

En Route Books and Media, LLC
5705 Rhodes Avenue
St. Louis, MO 63109

Cover credit: Sebastian Mahfood

ISBN-13: 979-8-88870-039-6
Library of Congress Control Number:
https://catalog.loc.gov/

Dedication

To the One God in Three, Who is. To my beloved parents, now with God, who introduced me to Jesus, raised me to love the Bible, and claimed Proverbs 22:6.

And to my professors and fellow travelers at Holy Apostles College & Seminary, where, with the grace of God, my faith coalesced such that I can say with certainty today, "I am Catholic."

CONTENTS

PREFACE

In May of 2021, I received a Master of Arts in Theology with a concentration in Church History from Holy Apostles College & Seminary, a Catholic liberal arts college located in Cromwell, CT, that offers online degree programs. The program took me five years to complete, and during that time I was active in an Evangelical church.

A year after my graduation, at the 2022 Easter Service, I entered into communion with the Roman Catholic Church. After five years of study, one year of contemplation, and a decades-long journey in search of the original New Testament Church, I reached my destination.

Born into a devoutly Fundamentalist Baptist home, and baptized at the age of six, I was raised to believe that Baptists practiced the truest form of New Testament Christianity. My father was a pastor, and my parents were both dedicated in their service to the Lord, and I could never thank them enough for my Bible-based upbringing. There came a time, however, when an inherited belief proved to be an insufficient foundation for life, if life was to be lived on a deeper level. The key words in the sentence above are "inherited belief," for to truly believe, one needs to personally understand one's faith beyond the superficial.

Some people do not question their spiritual heritage. Perhaps they truly do believe, or, as in my case, the beliefs were familiar and familial, comforting enough to sustain me until the need arose to substantiate my convictions to myself.

A good foundation must be uniform, level, and strong to properly support a structure. When the foundation of a building cracks, it is not safe to simply patch it up without knowing the cause of the fracture. To do so, or worse, to simply ignore the discovery, is potentially dangerous. The surety of the foundation, whether we speak of material buildings or physical lives, is critical if we hope to weather the storms of life.

The fractures in my inherited belief began with simple observations, followed by questions. The questions, largely unanswered, created more cracks in a vicious cycle of speculation and doubt that ultimately led to the collapse of my inherited foundation. All I had ever known turned to rubble, and to rebuild would mean establishing a new foundation that I could trust. This proved to be a challenge because at nineteen my knowledge was limited to the old foundation, which was now gone.

The quest for solid ground, to find an unshakable base on which to build my life, would lead me to places I did not want to go. I was like a child who finds herself lost in a forest as night begins to fall. Surrounded by blowing leaves and creaking branches, with fear my only companion, I hoped, for hope was all I had left. Then God, who is ever gracious and loving, took pity on this lost one by removing the darkness with the glowing lights of home. *Hope deferred makes the heart sick, but a wish fulfilled is a tree of life* (Proverbs 13:12).

This book is a personal story and not a work of theology, apologetics, or Church history, though excerpts from all are interwoven. It reflects a thought process, fueled by a complex spiritual journey where, at times, perseverance was my only hope.

In my travels, and with great quantities of time spent on discovery, I was able to conclude that the Catholic Church today is the successor of the Apostles and the continuation of the Church of the New Testament.

This is my story.

CHAPTER ONE

Growing up
Independent Fundamental Baptist

Pastor Curtis Lee Laws, an early 20th-century editor for the national Baptist paper <u>The Watchman-Examiner</u>, wrote a series of essays on *The Fundamentals* of core doctrinal belief between 1915-1920. His writings were inspired by the modernist incursion into historic Christian teachings. "Modernism" was the label applied to a developing school of thought grounded in hyper-criticism whereby some theologians, academics, and scholars placed Christianity's core tenets of faith under an empirical microscope.

The movement was influenced by 16th-and 17th-century philosophies that began to question our human ability to know and understand the world around us, and whether certain truth could be realistically grasped through our senses and intellect. Certain truth is defined here as "objective and absolute" in nature, form, and function.

With the tremendous progress of the physical and life sciences in the 18th and 19th centuries, the search for knowable truth, and the ability to find it, was increasingly defined by a narrow scientific methodology. What had originally started as a practical method of observation for investigating physical and biological sciences gradually shifted into all academic disciplines. Because of the surety that the scientific method was able to achieve, largely through evidentiary proof channeled through the sensory-based human mind, it became the new litmus test of all truth.

With the empirical method's becoming the diagnostic tool of all truth, some areas of study, such as the metaphysical nature of being, objective and universal ideas, and anything tied to the supernatural, were considered unknowable because they could not past the empirical test. Theology, once the "Queen of Sciences," along with epistemology (the study of the theory of knowledge) and ontology (the study of the nature of being) became subject to the rigors of the scientific method and quickly dethroned from the realm of certain knowledge.

As confidence in the scientific method grew, it dominated the definition of what could and could not be known. That which passed the litmus test could be certain, and that which did not, failed. This was a significant shift in knowledge and knowing, which, from this ultra-humanist perspective, rendered faith in God (or gods), celestial beings, miracles, and other "unexplainable" phenomena as unknowable. This marginalization of all things "unproven" because they (supposedly) lacked physical evidence began leaking into mainstream seminaries, which produced Christian theologians, ministers, and educators. Modernism posed a serious crisis within Christianity and her divine mandate to bring the Gospel to the world. If her faith is forcefully divorced from reason, then her certain truths, revealed by God through nature, the person of Jesus Christ, and Scripture may be dismissed, for they lack the requisite certainty science requires. And to dismiss knowledge of the supernatural meant gutting the faith, for if Christianity is stripped of her supernatural aspects, all that remains is a collection of moral teachings.[1]

††††

Though difficult to trace, it is possible that from Laws' essays the term "fundamentalist" was later adopted by many churches, including Baptists. By the 1920s, the modernist

---

[1] Modernism was not just a Protestant Problem; it had infected Catholicism as well. Pope Leo XIII (1878-1903) was dismayed by the emergence of heterodox teachings among some Catholic theologians, and his successor Pope Pius X would condemn modernism in his 1907 decree *Lamentabili* and encyclical *Pascendi*.

"alarm" had been raised and a countermovement ignited to defend the fundamentals of the faith, including her supernatural truths. That the world might embrace the burgeoning theory of evolution, replacing God as the Author of life, was alarming, but that these ideas were encroaching on the Christian faith, was unacceptable.

As counter-modernist teachings spread, they created divisions within the many Baptist Conventions. Congregational in polity, Baptists practice a form of decentralized church structure, with a Pastor as the head of the local church. Conventions, a form of loose association among local Baptist churches, often formed to support missionaries and later educational institutions.

The first Baptist Convention in the United States was the Triennial Convention incorporated in 1814. In 1845, the convention split into Northern Baptist and Southern Baptist, divided over the slavery issue. At the turn of the last century, other conventions existed as well, but the Northern and Southern were the two largest in America at the time. If a convention was large enough, and wealthy enough, it could support its own colleges to ensure Baptist education for ministers, missionaries, and teachers. For example, Baylor University was founded by the Baptist General Convention of Texas in 1845.

In the early 20th century, as Fundamentalism grew in influence, congregations were breaking away from their respective convention and began to call themselves "Independent Fundamental Baptists." And as the number of these churches increased, they would often form a loose coalition, typically called a "fellowship," of like-minded but strictly autonomous churches that rallied around the flag of common doctrine and practice. Often, these new fellowships served just that purpose, fellowship among pastors and congregations, and like their conventional predecessors, they also formed to support missionaries who were equally fundamental in ideology. Fellowships, as such, would be utilized to replace prior conventions as a clearing house for missionary support.

By the time I was born, Fundamental Baptist Fellowships were well established nationwide, and our particular group, the Baptist Bible Fellowship, had over 4,000 congregations. Our group had broken away from the World Baptist Fellowship in 1950, which had formed originally in 1933 when Texas firebrand, Pastor J. Frank Norris, was expelled from the Southern Baptist Convention. Norris, who was highly influential in Baptist circles, was able to encourage 150 pastors and their congregations to join him in forming a new fellowship.

The core ideology of these vocally independent and fundamental church fellowships consisted of a militant defense of both historic Christian teachings and specific Baptist beliefs. The Christian defense was against modernist teachings, such as denying the virgin birth of Jesus. The Baptist defense continued to maintain "believer's baptism" and the "priesthood of the believer." Along with these, they were devoted to the autonomy of the local church and adhered to the dispensational, pre-millennial system of Scriptural interpretation.

†††

The Anglo-Irishman John Nelson Darby (1800-1882), a trained lawyer who turned to the ministry, is considered to be the father of dispensationalism. By systematically dividing the Old and New Testaments into "dispensations," or definitive eras, Darby plotted a progressive and prophetic timeline that began with the Book of Genesis and ended with the Book of Revelation. The first dispensation was Paradise in Genesis, and the last is the future "Millennium," a period of 1,000 years when Christ will personally rule on earth, taken from the Book of Revelation. Dividing the Bible into eras was not original, yet the progressive nature of revelation and the premillennial aspect on future events were new and exciting developments.

A premillennialist, Darby believed that the earthly Church would be "raptured," that is to say, taken up into heaven, before the seven-year Tribulation that precedes Christ' millennial reign on earth. It is an eschatological (end-times) teaching that associates events in the Book of Revelation with the seventy weeks mentioned in the Old Testament Book of Daniel in chapter 9.

Darby's system of Scriptural interpretation gained momentum in America through the publication of the *Scofield Reference Bible* in 1909 and based upon the 1611 Authorized King James Version of the Bible, the premier translation used by Baptists. Rev. C.I. Scofield, a man of dubious integrity and education, applied Darby's dispensational and premillennial system throughout the Bible, adding his own chapter sub-divisions and commentary in the form of footnotes. His almost science-fiction interpretation of the Book of Revelation gained an immense following among Fundamentalists. The extent of his eschatological influence can be seen today in the highly successful book and film series "Left Behind" by Pastor Tim LaHaye, an apocalyptic piece of fiction grounded in dispensational premillennialism.

†††

As "Fundamentalism!" became the rallying cry for the act of separation from anything that appeared modernist, America witnessed an era of theological activism through periodicals, newspapers, lectures, and the creation of Bible institutes. Although conventions lacked true hierarchical power, they controlled their own colleges and publishing houses, and many of these were deemed as compromised by the early 1920s. Fundamentalists would have to blaze their own media and educational trails.

With the rise of the Fundamentalist Baptist churches, power was often concentrated in the hands of the pastor. The emphasis on Congregational polity, a movement within the original Reformation, where a local congregation is centered around one senior leader, is not unique to Baptists but a carryover from the "separatist" movements against State-sponsored churches, such as the Church of England. Christians who adhered to Congregationalism broke away from the Church of England's episcopal polity, whose structure closely resembled that of Roman Catholicism. Baptists, according to Landmarkism (discussed in chapter two), were always congregational in nature.

Episcopal polity is a traditional form of church governance, where a Bishop in charge of many churches in his diocese assigns a pastor or priest to a local church. This form of governance may be seen today within reformed denominations such as United Methodism and Lutheranism. Under episcopal polity, the local flock, and not the shepherd, is the central focus. This structure helps to ensure a unified standard of doctrine and practice for the denomination whose authority is more centralized. With congregational polity, however, a cult of personality surrounding a leader is easily fostered because, more often than not, one man (or woman) could become the "founder" of their church or movement. Without any institutional oversight, particularly in America, anyone could start a "church" or religious movement, and many did.

When an independent Baptist pastor, especially a vibrant orator, became prominent within his community, his congregation often grew around his persona. And at a time when Fundamentalism was on the rise, a church could quickly outgrow its physical building. It was the beginning of the modern mega-church movement, and as congregations swelled in size, some upwards of 10,000 for a Sunday service, Fundamentalist aspirations encouraged growth beyond the pews in an attempt to influence a greater portion of the population. Men such as Pastor John R. Rice of Texas began publishing The Sword of the Lord in 1934, handing out thousands of newspapers on the streets of Dallas. Even earlier than that, in the 1920s, the notorious J. Frank Norris, a Baptist pastor also from Texas known for his pulpit antics, published The Searchlight. As Fundamentalism gained in popularity, even a church newspaper, like The Searchlight, could draw secular advertisers such as J.C. Penny & Company.

Dedicated originally to the militant defense of the faith, these papers also supported the burgeoning movement for a "Christian America" by castigating non-sectarians as well as compromised sectarians for removing God from religion and society. It was during this same period that the contentious Scopes "Monkey" Trial (1925) pitted fundamentalism against Darwinism and became national headline news. Fundamentalism was being equated with the rising tide of *Americanism*, taking its anti-modernist, anti-evolutionist, and anti-communist message to the streets.

In addition to a pen-and-ink defense, the disdain for historic Congregationalist seminaries, such as Harvard and Princeton, as well as traditionally Baptist colleges, like Baylor, the 1930s and 1940s gave rise to Baptist Bible Institutes that would ensure an iron-clad Fundamental education for pastors, missionaries, and teachers. Like the highly successful newspapers, most of these new schools were linked directly to a large independent church with a prominent pastor. In 1939, J. Frank Norris' First Baptist Church of Arlington, Texas, founded the Fundamental Baptist Bible Institute. And just after World War II, in 1946, Tennessee Temple University was founded by Pastor Lee Roberson of the Highland Park Baptist Church in Chattanooga, Tennessee. My own father had graduated from Midwestern Baptist College, founded in 1953 by Pastor Tom Malone of Emmanual Baptist Church in Pontiac, Michigan. And perhaps the most well-known independent Baptist college to spring from the already mature movement was Lynchburg Baptist College (now Liberty University) established in 1971 by pastor Jerry Falwell and Thomas Road Baptist Church in Lynchburg, Virginia. These schools, and many others, graduated tens of thousands of pastors, missionaries, and educators who shunned modernism and were devoted to the fidelity of historic Baptist beliefs.

Growing up Baptist can be summed up in one simple phrase my father used to say, "The Bible says it, I believe it, and that settles it!" It was not as fancy as John Calvin's Latin *Sola Scriptura*, but the point was made. The Bible (excluding the deuterocanonical books) was the only true authority of the Church. We recognized no councils, creeds, or ecclesial hierarchy, but we believed in the literal interpretation of the Bible and practiced, or so I thought, the most genuine form of New Testament Christianity.

†††

While theological modernism was the newest enemy of the Fundamentalist movement, I need to spend a moment on an even older foe—Roman Catholicism. For much like modernist teachings, our churches never ceased to rail against Catholicism; it became an American pastime.

American history is filled with anti-Catholic prejudice from both doctrinal as well as cultural and political standpoints. Prior to American Independence, and even with the establishment of Catholic friendly Maryland by George Calvert (d. 1632), English Puritans held the minority Catholic population in contempt. Calvert's dream of a progressive community, where both Protestants and Catholics could worship freely, was constantly under attack as mainstream Protestants were not so like-minded.

After the American Revolution, and during the mid-19th century, the disdain for America's Catholic population only gained momentum as German and Irish Catholics flooded her shores. These refugees of European war and famine had left their homelands in hope of a fresh start in the fledgling democratic country that boasted of "life, liberty, and the pursuit of happiness." Sadly for them, it turned out to be a case of false advertising.

Historically, Catholics were theological antagonists, but by the early 1830s, Catholics were viewed by many as a growing threat to the "American" ideal held by authentic (i.e., non-Catholic) citizens. The supposed threat, driven by religious, political, and economic prejudice was not uncommonly manifested in acts of violence against immigrants and their property. In 1834, Boston saw the burning of the Ursuline convent, and ten years later, in 1844, the Philadelphia Bible riots broke out.

As the population of unwanted Catholics surged into the millions, American "Nativists" and their "Know-Nothings" political party waged a cultural war against everything outside their primarily Anglo-Saxon, Protestant circle. This was all too evident in 1855 when America witnessed Louisville's "Bloody Monday" battles where mobs of political "Know-Nothings" attacked German and Irish neighborhoods on election day.

By the turn of the 20th century, bigotry, if not outright hatred, for all immigrants (Catholic, Jewish, Asian, and even African-Americans migrating North) had inflamed the country. Much to my personal dismay, some Baptists played no small part fueling the movement of a white and Protestant America.

At its peak in the 1920s, Americanism was sweeping the nation. With the blockbuster release of *The Birth of a Nation* in 1915, the "old" south partnered with a rising northern wave of anti-immigration sentiment. Within a few years, the Ku Klux Klan would be revived at a national level, gaining millions of members primarily in the north (New York and Pennsylvania) and mid-West (Indiana and Ohio). Originally grounded in the anti-African American, pro-Jim Crow South, this newly revised group expanded their hatred to include anyone that did not fit into their mold. One such promoter of the Nativist ideal was Rev. C. Lewis Fowler (1877-1974), a Baptist pastor and college president from Atlanta. Fowler praised the new KKK in a 1922 pamphlet entitled The Ku Klux Klan: Its Origin, Meaning and Scope of Operation, where the preface states:

> The Author sincerely hopes this work will
> make a contribution to real Americanism,
> to American Protestantism, and that it may
> develop the patriots in our land.

Subsequent to this, Fowler had also written two other pamphlets entitled Rome - A Menace to Modern Civilization and <u>The Jew - A Menace to Modern Civilization</u>. Now, Fowler wasn't the only Baptist Pastor, or even Christian leader, riding the wave of bigotry. There was plenty of blame to go around the denominational block. The fact that he was BAPTIST, however, particularly bothered me. It bothered me because that was not how I was raised, yet it was part of Baptist history.

I thank God that I was brought up by a Baptist Pastor who did not embrace that type of grotesque bigotry. My prejudiced upbringing remained strictly theological in content.

†††

Implicit or explicit, the unifying belief among Baptists was that the Roman Catholic Church was the "harlot of Babylon," referenced in Revelation 17:5.[2] According to the Reformation that swept through Europe and England in the 16th century, the Roman Catholic Church was viewed

---

[2] The popularization of this phrase traditionally originated with Peter Waldo (d. 1218), who was a wealthy merchant from Lyons who became the leader of his own ascetic sect the "Poor Men of Lyons," later called "Waldensians," that separated from the Catholic Church. They are considered in the lineage of Baptist Succession Theory.

as a corruption of biblical Christianity. Baptists developed late in the evolution of the Reformation, officially breaking from the Church of England around 1600. Yet like their predecessor separatists, such as the Puritans, they too adopted the same anti-Catholic sentiment and brought it with them to the colonies.

Ultimately becoming the largest non-Catholic denomination in America, Baptists in the 20th century could read from their *Scofield Reference Bible*, anti-Catholic theological footnotes such as "Ecclesiastical Babylon is all apostate Christendom, in which the Papacy will undoubtedly be prominent," noted in Revelation 18:2. While the Bible was acknowledged as the only authority for the Christian faith, Scofield's notes were taken as gospel truth and millions of Americans trusted, and still trust in, his premillennial and dispensational anti-Catholic commentary.

This 500-year-old theological vitriol against the Catholic Church has never ceased and can be seen today even in comic book form. I remember as a kid in the 1970s reading colorful tracts by cartoonist Jack Chick. Chick Publications, founded in 1961 in Rancho Cucamonga, California, produced (and still produces) comic books with anti-Catholic themes. They are considered "evangelistic" tools intended to scare people away from Catholicism, which is presented as rife with false doctrine and occultism. As a child in the 1970s, I knew nothing about the Roman Catholic Church or her theology, but my comic books convinced me that it was the devil's church and that the Pope was the anti-Christ.

†††

From childhood through my teenage years, I believed everything I was taught. My upbringing afforded me a sense of security from which I could understand the world around me, and on more than one occasion it provided me with confidence in the public school system. By then the word "fundamentalist" was in the early stages of being redefined as pejorative, but my parents taught me that it was never wrong to be on the side of right, even if it meant standing alone among my peers. Independence, fundamentalism, and separation were badges of merit.

Early in high school, I felt that God had called me to serve in foreign missions. My mother and father were in full-time ministry, and their passion for missions was contagious. With my father being a pastor, there were many instances where I found myself at the dinner table with someone who spoke Korean or Swahili. Between my parents and my admiration for missionaries, I assumed working in ministry was a natural next step. The idea certainly wasn't farfetched as we had no less than eight ordained ministers in the family, with my older brother and several cousins attending Baptist Bible colleges. Like Lt. Dan in *Forrest Gump*, who believed he was destined to die on the battlefield, I believed I was destined to serve on the mission field. Through myopic and very rose-tinted glasses, I saw our family as a dynasty, taking the true version of the New Testament Gospel to the world. It was the daydream of a teenager, whose naïveté would be jolted just beyond the threshold of college.

CHAPTER TWO

Breaking News!
Bible Student turns Agnostic

It was a thrill to leave home at 18 and venture to a college that would be filled with like-minded young people all seeking to "go forth and serve" the Lord under the Fundamentalist Baptist flag. My school was at its peak, with nearly 2,000 men and women training in various programs that fell into four major categories: education, missions, music, and pastoral ministries. Because all the degrees were oriented toward ministry, there were no traditional majors, such as history or psychology, and subsequently, the school was unaccredited. This mattered little to us at the time, for accreditation was non-essential to our ministerial goal. Only that which practically applied to our ministry, such as English and public speaking, were considered as necessary, non-biblical coursework.

The 24/7 atmosphere, which included our living in dorms, praying and eating and studying together, should have been a spiritually safe place for a missionary-in-progress, yet by the end of my first year, in the belly of all things fundamentally Baptist, I began to question my beliefs.

The catalyst for the hair-line cracks that formed my freshman year was a course in Church History. The class, heavily influenced by both Reformation and Baptist perspective, should have been a reinforcement of my life-long faith. It would be a formal introduction to a subject matter that was not taught in public school or Sunday school. Yet in this academic setting, with a PhD leading the class,[3] the more I listened the less certain I became. It was not any one thing I could pinpoint at the time, but *something* was not quite right.

As the course progressed that first year, I began to perceive inaccuracies that could not otherwise be substantiated; like a gut feeling that lacks evidence. And while I had no point of reference to make a legitimate case for doubt—my prior knowledge of Church history was nil—I was compelled to ask questions. Believing there was no such thing as a stupid question, I raised my hand on several occasions and discovered quickly that there *are* stupid

---

[3] This is important to note because, at the time, highly educated people were often considered suspect among Baptists because they might be contaminated by the world, or modernism. As such, Bible Colleges preferred Pastors and former Missionaries as educators.

questions. It was not my "but what about?" ignorance that dismayed the professor (he could anticipate that in a freshman); rather, it was the act of questioning what was considered unquestionable. In raising my hand, I had innocently tripped over the *status quo* of Baptist dogma and could sense the pupils of my classmates dilating. Unsure of what I had done wrong, but thoroughly embarrassed, I was dissuaded from further public inquiry. Unlike at home, where my parents patiently answered my multiple "whys" as a child, my new home was a forum where learning was more rote than thoughtful.

The many questions that popped into my head and remained there unanswered led to speculation and doubt. What could have been a simple hesitation in faith, had it been dealt with early on, became disproportionately complicated by the end of that first year. I needed answers, but as the subject of a monocratic theological institution, I could not risk being labeled a liberal or worse, a modernist, by simply asking questions. Had this been the 2020s, I could have fallen back on internet investigating, but this was the early 1980s and we were still reading physical books and using electric type-writers.

Internalizing questions left unanswered did more than simply provoke doubt, it robbed me of the sense of security that I found in my upbringing. Whatever confidence I had when I entered college was now replaced by an awkward insecurity, as I began to realize that my beliefs were not mine at all. I believed because my parents believed. I believed because it was what I was taught. I believed because I knew no other way. And even though I still knew no other way, for there was nothing to compare and contrast my beliefs against, my foundation started to crumble. Caught completely off-guard, I found myself in mid-life crisis. I had become some Shakespearean character in a tragedy, asking *Who am I?* and *What on earth just happened?* One year into college, at the age of nineteen, an abyss normally reserved for later in life swallowed me whole.

†††

As a child who grew up reading everything in sight, including cereal boxes, I had developed a fascination with thinking about what I read. In high school, this made me a good student, as I normally went beyond what was required to understand *more*. I wasn't the kid who took clocks apart, but I enjoyed parsing words and understanding their origin. Unfortunately, this sense of inquiry had never crept up regarding my home-spun faith; it was what it was, and I had accepted it at face value.

Now, no longer a child but a young adult away at college, I began to examine Reformation history, taking it apart to see what it was made of. Instead of understanding, however, the more I dissected ideas the more doubts accumulated. In a library heavily bent toward fundamentalism, it was not easy to grasp a holistic view of Church history; parts were obviously missing. And the intentional marginalization, if not complete exclusion, of the Catholic contribution to Christian history only served to pique my interest.

Though I was not educated in post-apostolic history, I knew Catholics traced themselves back to the Apostles; Peter was the first Pope, or so the Catholics said. I also knew that the Reformation began approximately 1,500 years *after* Christ. These things did not stack up against what I was being taught. The theory of Baptist successionism, a concept based on 19th-century "Landmarkism," was a popular topic. This concept, heavily influenced by the 1931 publication *Trail of Blood* by pastor J.M. Carroll (Appendix II "Trail of Blood Timeline") espoused historical links between Baptists and 1st-century Christians by tracing common beliefs through various "Christian" groups that were always outside the Catholic Church. The idea of a continuous line of "believers" running parallel to the Catholic

Church and later Reformation was an attempt to supplant the Catholic teaching of Apostolic Succession.

As my education continued into my sophomore year, I found myself outwardly submitting to my professors, but inwardly I was confused and not a little frightened. I had not returned home the summer prior—jobs were scarce—so I stayed with relatives in Texas who found me full-time work. The occasion to speak in-depth with my parents, whom I trusted with my life, had passed me by. I am not sure if I would have confided in them, but I do know that things only worsened without them.

Back in school my sophomore year, each passing week darkened my spirit which manifested in lack of interest and declining grades. My freshman enthusiasm had been replaced with a gloomy attitude, frequently displayed by sarcasm. The pent-up skepticism that was brewing inside began to spill out, and fellow students, now friends, took notice. For every concerned "What's wrong?" there was a quick "Nothing" in reply. Sometimes, I even pawned my moods off on the Devil, the known enemy of Bible college students, but I knew it wasn't all about him. This was not about temptation, but a crisis of faith.

††††

During the prior summer, as I worked in Texas, I had prayed to God in earnest about my confusion. I recall getting on my knees beside my bed and asking God for help, and each time I went to sleep feeling neither consolation nor clarification. It was as if God "wasn't home," and that, above all things, disturbed me because I thought God and I were close. With no one to turn to, and God not seeming to listen, I was convinced there was something wrong with me.

By my junior year, everything came to a head as I witnessed the ground completely give way beneath my feet. Going through the motions, with nothing to stand on, I floated in disbelief and became increasingly depressed and ashamed. The final straw was mid-term, when my best friend said we could not be friends anymore. He had been my last bridge to spiritual sanity, and with the collapse of our friendship the camel's back finally broke. I called my bewildered parents and begged to come home.

My attempt to understand church history had led to questioning not only my Baptist beliefs, but also the validity of Christianity, and the very existence of God. In two and a half years my faith had changed to unfaith, and, ironically, there had not been a modernist influencer in sight. Through my own curiosity, I had become an involuntary agnostic. In the truest sense of the word, I no longer knew what to believe, so I believed nothing.

CHAPTER THREE

The Roundabout: Looking for an Exit

Roundabouts, or as we call them in America "traffic circles," are more common in Europe than in America; there are over 60,000 in France alone versus our less than 10,000. They are considered a safer and more efficient method of controlling a busy intersection. A driver enters the circle and drives around until they find their exit. The process is simple enough, but it can be confusing to the novice driver who might concentrate more on the continual flow of traffic entering and exiting, than on their target exit. And what happens to the driver who does not know which exit to take? They keep going in circles.

After dropping out of college and returning home, I found myself in a spiritual roundabout. The original exit, my calling to the mission field, was now blocked, and the lack of a contingency plan had left me without an alternate route. I was a college drop-out, living with the folks again, miserable and lacking a compass to guide me.

It is difficult to describe how dark that time was, especially in contrast to just two years prior when I was filled with enthusiasm. The real me, or the me I remember, had slowly disappeared. Where that person had gone, I wasn't sure, but to survive my homecoming, I had to put on a façade of my former self. No one else, especially my loving parents, needed to know how bad things had become. Though they may have suspected something was wrong, I could not begin to formulate all that had happened; too much water had passed underneath that bridge. I was now in survival mode, quickly putting the past away, and asking myself, "What am I going to do now?" Ironically, as one who enjoys thinking, I was beginning to understand why Baptists were typically anti-intellectual. Thinking had brought me nothing but heartache and confusion.

In the following months, this PK (pastor's kid) faked belief just to get through each day after arriving home. Attending services each Sunday morning and evening, as well as mid-week prayer meetings, I accompanied my parents with Bible in hand. The sacred book no longer meant much and had become little more than an accessory. With daily life a cyclical trap, the need to escape became my only thought. The key was becoming independent and getting out of the house. The first step toward that goal was a part-time job and a fresh start at education. As mentioned previously, the Bible college I had attended was unaccredited, which meant no coursework was transferable, and, once again, at the age of twenty-one, I was a freshman taking rudimentary classes.

The new routine of work and school provided some consolation from the inner chaos. There was still no compass, no real goal other than independence at this point, but during that first year living at home I had begun to work out some internal issues. I accepted responsibility for some of my actions; not that anyone else was to blame at that point. It was my decision to go to Bible college and my decision to drop out. It was my decision to not discuss anything with my parents, but to play the role of a hypocrite, returning to my father's church as a "closet" unbeliever. Yet in all this, there was one thing that I had not been able to accept—agnosticism. Becoming a non-believer was an unplanned consequence of my questions and doubts, and I resented existing in this involuntary state.

††††

Within a year's time, I moved away from my parents. When the opportunity to relocate to Southern California arrived, I took advantage of it, eager to lose the hypocritical baggage shouldered every week for the past twelve months. I loved my parents dearly, but by getting out of the house and placing 600 miles between us, I could finally be free of my false persona by no longer attending church.

Over the course of the next two years, working and taking classes to fulfill core requirements, yet still lacking a major or career objective, my unbelief remained constant. Though I tried not to think about it, my unspiritual state continued to trouble me. Christianity was no longer my foundation, but there was no solace found in its replacement. As far as I was concerned, agnosticism was intellectual neutrality; it offered no definitive answers regarding metaphysics or the meaning of life. The idea of "neither believing nor disbelieving" propelled me in circles, and I continued to hope for something other than this to build a life on. I had read about agnostics who embraced the certainty of being uncertain but could not accept their fence-straddling conclusions. A state of perpetual detachment, whether voluntary or involuntary, from the "why" of existence is not a foundation— it's limbo. I had more respect for theists and atheists who held knowledge they considered certain. There had to be an alternative to the shifting sands of agnosticism, and I would not rest until it was found.

†††

The search for alternatives was secondary to work and school, which bolstered me through a normal day, but when the occasion rose to check out this "school of thought" or that "religion," I would investigate. The detail of each other-worldly inquiry is unnecessary and would probably be quite boring, but I will say that the metaphysical exits encountered on the spiritual roundabout were brightly lit and often backed up with a heavy flow of traffic. Other people were searching, too, and, like myself, they could not accept the fatalism of an existence born from an exclusively materialistic standpoint. There had to be more.

As I investigated the variety of other-worldly systems of belief, the end result was typically the same—a dead end. Each promising exit, so heavily trafficked by fellow humans, either led to some form of ego-centrism or cosmic impersonalism. It was either all about me, or nothing about me. And with every hopeful exit taken, the desire to find a sure foundation was deferred.

As I scratched off each possible exit from the now nauseating roundabout, the idea that the meaning I longed for, the "why" of my life, grew more elusive. If this quest to find meaning in life beyond the purely physical realm could not be manifested in reality, then I would be faced with fatalism, and at that thought I cringed. In the same way as the television character Fox Mulder (The X-Files) wanted to believe that the truth was out there—so did I. Of course, the truth that I was looking for was not proof of extra-terrestrials, or even the origin of human life – I was content to have come from my mother and father – it was about the whole *purpose of being*. Fox was the true modern agent, caring about the "what and how," but I was still in the "why" mode, and modern science no longer cared to answer that intangible question.

†††

It is so very true that "hope deferred makes the heart sick," and as the years passed by on that roundabout my heart was heading toward terminal illness. Only then, on the brink of giving up, did I notice another exit. Overshadowed by the glitz and magnitude of the other signs, it was made of simple wood and read "The Narrow Way." My heart nearly went into arrythmia as I recognized that road. The Narrow Way was the road I had taken to the traffic circle in the first place, five years earlier. No time was wasted as I put on my turn signal and took the exit.

For all the explorations, and subsequent dead ends, I was back—reinvestigating Christianity. This time, however, I was able to compare what I had learned on the round-about against the faith of my childhood, and in doing so, I realized that only Christianity could adequately answer the question of "why am I?" And it wasn't just about believing because I wanted too, but because Christianity made sense. Five years after entering the circle of uncertainty, looking for the most basic answer to the meaning of life, it was the old road, paved by the cross of Christ, that satisfied me. "Hope deferred makes the heart sick, but when the desire comes, it is a tree of life" (Proverbs 13:12).

The end?

Not quite.

CHAPTER FOUR

Back to Square One, *Generally Speaking*

By now it may be obvious to the reader that I am an overthinker, and you would be right. Everything I attempted during those years of confusion was heavily pondered and although I had re-discovered the Christian faith, my thinking wasn't over. I had gained knowledge, but not wisdom; both of which, and not simply thinking, are spiritual gifts. Falling short of wisdom, the story only gets worse.

Barely a few miles into the exit, and traveling along the Narrow Way, my thoughts stirred as I looked over the familiar territory. This lonely road, with its bumps and potholes, elicited memories. Flashbacks of unhappy times obscured my view and stirred up a mental dust storm. The terrain was no longer pleasing to the eye, and what could have been a happy ending, complete with balloons, a fatted calf and me running into the arms of God, disappeared into a cloud of growing discontent. The initial relief, the sweet reminiscence of childhood security, was being swept away by more recent recollections that, as I dwelled on them, altered my attitude. I was traveling back down the *very road* that had led to my spiritual demise and asking, "How can a road lead both to and from confusion, and more importantly, why did it happen?

Reflecting back on years of believing, not believing, and believing again, I asked, "Was this all necessary, just to bring me back to square one?" Seriously? The paradox of the road, the whole drama of the journey, eviscerated my short-lived reunion. Even in attempting to emphasize the positive – rediscovering Christianity – the negative aspects of the ordeal overwhelmed me. I had become jaded, and the more I thought about it, the less I cared. Everything about this scenario was wrong.

Before Bible college I had been a fun person, leading an unquestioned, if not oblivious, life. I loved Jesus and my parents and my church and my friends, and I really enjoyed laughter. Five years later, as an adult, there was nothing funny about this situation. At the beginning of the whole charade, I was angry with myself for having doubted and questioned my Baptist faith, but now I became irritated with God whom I began to suspect had interrupted my child-like faith by putting me through a spiritual wringer. To him I directed, less a question than an accusation, "How could you do this to me?" And, more importantly, "Why?" The more I asked, the more the anger increased until I finally told him, "I did not deserve this." And I was so certain of that fact that I began to build a case against God.

As judge, jury, and attorney, my argument was simple and straight forward. Fact No. 1: I had been an obedient child. Fact No. 2: I had willingly submitted to a call to ministry. Fact No. 3: God chained me to chaos for five years. It was a cruel and unusual penalty for one who had broken no laws. My concluding argument was, "How could the all-knowing, all-seeing, all-loving Father have punished me with doubt, angst, and dread for years of my irreplaceable youth, only to bring me back to the beginning of my faith?" It was unconscionable. Case closed.

By the time I had concluded my case against God, I had traveled a good distance away from the spiritual roundabout. Still traveling on the Narrow Way with confusion well behind me, I found myself tapping the brakes. The intellectual storm had passed, the spiritual sky had cleared, and I pulled my car over to the shoulder. Stepping out of the driver's side, I handed the keys to Jesus. Not only could he "take the wheel," he could have the whole car. I was done. I had returned to Christianity, in the fullest sense of faith and trust, only to walk away indifferent.

†††

Exhaustion is a common trait that can strike when overdue. It can make us physically ill, mentally tired, and emotionally disjointed. And if we are not careful, the effects of fatigue can damage relationships.

By the time I handed Jesus the keys, I was tired on every human level, and the extent of my exhaustion led to an anger that damaged my reunion with the Lord. In those years, from eighteen to twenty-three, the vicious cycle of disappointment, hope, and more disappointment had changed me. I knew I was not okay, but I was also convinced that God was not okay either.

†††

Though my anger toward God, and myself, would pass, it lasted long enough to be an impetus for change. In walking away, I had acquired a new foundation as a "believing but non-practicing Christian." That would be sufficient; there was no need to travel any further on God's straight and narrow. What I needed was a new road, paved by my own design.

In order to recapture some semblance of *joie de vivre,* my focus shifted from spiritual concerns to practical action. And to blaze this new trail would mean pulling myself up by my own bootstraps. It was time to be accountable for my actions, my way, and I had a tool perfect for the job: the Protestant work ethic. Max Weber's academic study on "duty" called and I answered.[4] This new plan would focus time and energy on the practical, and help me to regain the dignity that had been lost to utterly non-productive time. I had a lot of catching up to do.

At twenty-three, most of my peers had graduated college and started their lives of marriage and career-building. I was well in arrears. To catch up with where I thought I should be, I took a full-time office job and returned to night school at an accredited public university. Able to support myself, and with a goal of finally obtaining an undergraduate degree, my niche was found in a 70-hour work week.

---

[4] Maximilian Weber (1864-1920), a German sociologist and political economist, was one of the most influential theorists of the Western world. His essay, *The Protestant Ethic and the Spirit of Capitalism,* sought to trace the industrial age phenomena of productivity, as duty, to Reformation ethics.

Between work and school, both undergraduate and graduate, I was able to accrue a marketable skill-set and an education that would turn into a rewarding career. Though not intrinsically spiritual, hard work was part of my Christian heritage, and I was an heir to an ethic tied to duty and productivity. My parents were depression-era babies who understood what it meant to live hand-to-mouth and the importance of duty to one's self, family, work, and country. They embraced personal responsibility, and I admired them for that. They were real adults, and in the coming years I, too, would become a *bona fide* member of the "God helps those who help themselves" society.

The result of this metamorphosis was nothing short of spectacular as my career exceeded expectations. I did not climb the corporate ladder; *I skipped rungs* to positions of rank and remuneration. The motivation was never about money or position, though they were both quite nice, but the pride that comes with self-esteem. The years that had been wasted in spiritual limbo, with nothing to show for it externally, had resulted in a feeling of unworthiness. But with productivity—a measurable achievement—there was satisfaction. I earned those college degrees. I worked hard for this or that position. And work, for the sake of work, was my new calling. I had done it my way, and succeeded.

CHAPTER FIVE

The Definitive Crossroad

In my early forties, my beloved father died. Unlike many bombastic preachers with whom he fellowshipped, my father was a quiet man. Proclaiming the same fundamental truths as his peers, my father could draw people to him with a genuine spirit of charity. He was a thoughtful and congenial servant of the Lord, and he liked people. Despite Baptist history, swollen with prejudice, my Father always stressed the importance of "standing in another person's shoes." Mom and Dad both had been my Rock of Gibraltar, the only earthly home I ever knew, and now my father had terminal cancer. For the first time in twenty years, I found myself talking to God.

In the decades since I had given Jesus back the keys and walked away, there had been no communication with God. My judgment of him, and my choice to blaze my own trail, had been definitive. Yet, as my father's health declined, I approached God. There was no expectation that he would hear me for my sake, but I hoped he would listen on behalf of my father. My father, who had his own challenges in ministry and post-ministry, was devoted to his Savior, Jesus Christ. I had been a life-long witness.

†††

Two weeks after I had finally earned my undergraduate degree, I helped my folks move out of California and back to the Midwest where they both originated. In the years since I had left home, my parents and I had grown closer together, though they knew I no longer attended Church. Much like God, who never interfered with my chosen path, they were quick to praise my accomplishments but were quiet about my lack of spirituality. I knew it was not lack of concern; they always prayed for me, claiming Proverbs 22:6, "Train up a child in the way he should go and, when he is old, he will not depart from it."

After they relocated, I would visit them as often as possible and always around the holidays. During those visits, and without fail, I recall how each morning, when I would stumble toward the coffee maker, there would be an open Bible, a plate of toast crumbs, and an empty coffee mug on the kitchen table. Ever the early riser, my father had already eaten, read, and prayed. It had been his morning routine since I could remember.

In the months that led up to my father's death, I petitioned God for six requests. I asked him to take my Dad in the spring, his favorite time of year, and that he be surrounded by loved ones, though we all lived far away. I also asked if I could be there during his final days, both while he was still conscious and also at the moment of his death. And I asked that he pass without pain.

About a month after my father's funeral and my return to work, I realized that all six requests had been answered by God. Coincidence? Maybe, but those were very specific requests, and I believed it was God. Pride and gratefulness do not mix well, and though I had been distant for decades, God had heard me on behalf of my father and I was sincerely thankful. As momentous as this event was, it did not usher in an immediate reunion, yet between the death of my dad and the graciousness of God, a season of reflection began as I contemplated my life in the light of mortality.

††††

By American standards I was successful. With determination and an excellent education, I had built a rewarding career that included all the perquisites. Work I enjoyed, a beautiful home, nice car, and money in the bank that allowed me to splurge on family, friends, and myself; it was the definition of earthly contentment. The only real price I paid to achieve and maintain this lifestyle was to ignore the spiritual void that resulted in my separation from God. If I thought about him, it was a rare event, and frankly, I convinced myself that God was okay with my chosen path because he never bothered me after I left him. He was still there, I knew, but he never intruded upon my will, and that was fine with me. Let bygones be bygones. And if there were times that I thought I heard God's distant voice, it was easy to ignore; my interior voice—boosted by self-satisfaction—was much louder. With my father's death, however, which weighed heavily on my heart, I found myself turning down the volume of self-esteem. There was a creeping sense of diminishing returns on the skills, work ethic, and education I so highly valued.

†††

Where I live today, among undulating hills of farmland dotted by pretty barns of red or white, auctions are frequent and popular. These days, the children of farmers often leave for college and the city life, only to return when mom and dad have passed away or retire to a warmer climate. As such, these auctions are packed with generations of antiques and collectibles, something for every bidder. It's amazing to see what some people will collect, from stone jars to classic cars. While many attendees shop for items which bring them joy, others look for investment; hoping an old sausage grinder will appreciate in value one day. Like those collectors, I, too, had a showcase that was filled to the brim, but instead of figurines or model trains, my cabinet was bursting with hours of productivity.

After my father's death, I looked more closely at my collection, and the overall satisfaction began to wane. The college diplomas, the bank account, the material possessions, and the career promotions took on a new appearance. What I had collected was "stuff." It was all nice stuff, and it made me feel great for a long time, but it was just *stuff*. As I looked over my valuables, I could hear one of my father's favorite phrases, "You never see a hearse with a U-Haul trailer behind it." After twenty years, I was staring into my collectibles cabinet and wondering, "Is this all I possess?"

There is no shame in working hard and owning nice things, but it occurred to me that I had ended up as a cog in my own machine, after scoffing at the egocentric and materialist ideals decades prior. Other than praying for my father, a spiritual thought hadn't crossed my mind since I left Jesus back at the car, but now I was contemplating on that level once again. In working for the sake of work, fulfilling some sense of duty to be a productive individual, I had shelved the true "why" of my existence—to know and love God. Initiated by the impermanence of a life so dear, my "collectibles" turned to junk as I weighed the consequences of my rebellious lifestyle against the scales of eternity. I was a mortal denying my immortality, and though I had not "sold my soul," per se, I had willfully shoved it so far down inside that it would not interfere with my plans.

Like Oscar Wilde's character Dorian in *The Picture of Dorian Gray*, who in curiosity gazed upon his hidden and deformed portrait, I too looked upon the portrait of my soul. It had been clearly neglected. Unlike Dorian, however, who chose to hide his heinous picture and return to his life of debauchery, I retrieved my soul and brought it into the light. It required extensive cleaning.

†††

My father had died in the month of May, and in the autumn of that same year, when book stores were still numerous, I pursued a favorite pastime of browsing for a good read. As I passed a bargain table my eyes caught sight of a book entitled *The Purpose Driven Life*, written by Rick Warren, an Evangelical Pastor who lived near me. The book claimed to have sold over 20 million copies. Perhaps it was a good read, I was not sure, but it was discounted 50% so I bought it. It was just an ordinary day, in an ordinary place, that would bring extraordinary results. For shortly after my purchase, as I began to read, I found myself at a crossroad. A sign read:

> *Continue down the worldly way spiritually*
> *destitute, or return to The Narrow Way.*

The same day I opened the book, I found myself praying to God, only this time it was for me. Alone, and sitting at the dining room table, I said, "Lord, I want to come home." What followed next was a flood of sorrow co-mingled with joy impossible to describe. The one I had left had never left me, and not only that, he wanted me back! There were still no balloons or fatted calf, but this time I did run into my heavenly Father's arms.

†††

Making the right decision that October day was not difficult because God's timing is perfect. I had willingly played the role of a prodigal child, and he waited for my return. God was truly the welcoming Father who had never forsaken me. There would be no more running away, no more doing things my way, and I fully understood the ramifications of that decision—forfeiting my ego and replacing it with the mind and heart of Christ. Shortly after my spiritual return, I began to read an old devotional I had picked up in a London bookshop entitled *The Imitation of Christ* by Thomas à Kempis. I had purchased it when I was collecting little old books, never intending to actually read it, but now the title struck me. With my mind settled, the next issue that presented itself was implementing my return to church. Not only did I need to attend church, I wanted to, but was faced with the question "Where do I worship?"

CHAPTER SIX

Denominational Consumerism

Had I simply been a lapsed Fundamentalist Baptist, I could have embraced the faith of my childhood and ended my story here, yet I was no longer convinced that Fundamentalist Baptists were the genuine New Testament Church they claimed to be. Searching for a replacement church posed a whole new dilemma as I was now confronted by so many choices within Protestantism.

Imagine that you have eaten oatmeal for breakfast your entire life because your mom did the shopping and cooking. For all you knew, all moms buy oatmeal for breakfast. Then one day your mom sends you to the store to buy more oatmeal, and you discover a cereal aisle with a hundred choices. This was my predicament, for denominationally speaking, there were so many varieties and I had little clue which to choose.

As a by-product of the Reformation, today's "church aisle" has a multitude of denominations, sects, and, sadly, even cults. Reformers, such as Luther, Calvin, and Zwingli, who originally broke away from the Catholic Church in the

16th century, were never on the same page doctrinally speaking. They were united in their rebellion against Rome, but divided amongst themselves. And their initial protest would quickly bring disjointed ideas of both theological and practical "protest" within their own ranks and set a precedence for a Protestant mitosis where one sect breaks into two and two break into four and so on. Unlike cellular mitosis, where the "mother" cell is divided into equivalent "daughter" cells, with the purpose of unified reproduction, this ecclesial division achieved the opposite; no two sects were alike.

The original friction and discord among the Reformers ushered in an era of radically autonomous theological concepts and ecclesial ideals. Everything from the doctrine of grace to the structure of the church was disputed. Freedom from Rome gave way to liberty heretofore unseen, and this freedom has manifested in a never-ending ideology of Protestant separation. That Luther, Calvin, and Zwingli did not agree in the early stages of the reform movement is an example of how congregations formed around their own teachers. And, in time, a portion of one denomination would break away from their original source. A recent example of this is the newly formed Global Methodist Church, which broke away from the United Methodist Church in 2022, which separated from the Methodist

Episcopal Church in 1939, that had severed ties with the Church of England in 1795, which originally broke from the Roman Catholic Church in 1534. Five hundred years later, and the schisms just keep coming.

While non-Catholic followers of Jesus Christ use the umbrella term of "Christian," this title is as close as they come in regard to a true unity of faith and doctrine. Yet this unity of faith, in mind and body, is a core requisite of the Church (Phil. 2:1-5, I Peter 3:8), and not a substitute for the Antiochian label "Christian." That so many non-Catholic Christians are diverse in doctrine is contrary to Scripture, and this became my problem.

†††

As my search for a church began, which had only excluded Baptists at that point, I noticed two striking changes that had occurred since I last worshipped with a local congregation. First, a different atmosphere pervaded the worship service; second, there appeared to be a shift away from the importance, and subsequent practice, of historic doctrines.

The last time I had attended church, the pastor wore a suit and tie, folks dressed nicely, and there was a choir. The mood was both respectful and joyful. What I found now, however, were pastors wearing blue jeans, folks dressing in shorts and flip-flops, and the choir replaced by a "worship team" complete with drums and electric guitars. I knew society and technology had changed, for I had changed with it, but I was not expecting these changes to impact the way in which God was worshipped. It sounds like a superficial observation, even to me, but this new "coffee house and jam session" atmosphere appeared less dignified. And after reading a t-shirt that said, "Jesus is my homie," I could not help but feel that worship had become less respectful.

The next thing I noticed, and this was far more important, was the apparent marginalization of historical Christian teaching in both faith and morals. In some instances, the change was not obvious, it had to be discovered in the bylines of a church's statement of faith and practice, which of course I read because I am an obnoxious reader. In other churches, however, it was more an in-your-face experience of public defiance against Christian orthodoxy. Modernism, the fear of my father's era, had appeared to not only infect the Protestant denominations, but morphed into an ideology in practice that sidelined doctrine and welcomed subjectivism. It was a "Rip Van Winkle" awakening.

Washington Irving's story-book character Rip Van Winkle awoke from a twenty-year sleep and found that the

American revolution had come and gone. A drastic change for a man who had fallen asleep during the reign of King George III only to wake up to President George Washington, who had been elected by citizens. When I awoke from my spiritual nap, I found a revolution had taken place as well—a Christian revolution, where the objective and traditional truths of the New Testament had been replaced with idiosyncratic teachings. The God who IS love was replaced by a heterodox love of self. While I slept, a flock of revolutionary Christian sheep had revolted against their Monarch, King Jesus, and replaced him with elected sycophants. I seriously contemplated going back to sleep.

Of course, I could not go back to sleep but had to face the denominational cereal aisle and pick one to replace my oatmeal. As I scoured the ingredients of each denomination, hoping to find a church that, at the very least, held doctrinally orthodox teachings, the list was shortened, yet still too long to make an immediate decision.

†††

As I had mentioned above, regarding the Reformation genesis of Protestant denominationalism, America today has no shortage of ecclesial variety. There are older de-

nominations, such as Episcopal, Presbyterian, and Lutheran as well as others who developed later, such as Baptists and Pentecostals. Along with those groups there were
also congregations labeled "non-denominational," or "in-
ter-denominational." It was confusing as churches had become an American commodity branding themselves for
marketing purposes to attract Christian shoppers to their
product by appealing not only to superficial differences,
but orthodox as well. Understanding the source and consequence of congregational variety did not help me in my
search because I wasn't looking for cereal. I was looking for
the New Testament Church and beginning to wonder if
that particular brand had been discontinued.

†††

The search ended when I joined a local Evangelical
Church. It was a large congregation with a pastor who was
respected in my community. The fit was simply okay as I
was still saddened by the lack of unity among Christians
and yet knew I had to belong somewhere. There was no
sense in searching further; I acquiesced out of sheer neces-
sity to be part of a local congregation and remain obedient
to the faith.

The good news, and this truly is good news, was that by attending church regularly, and reading my Bible daily, a desire to learn "all things biblical" was reignited. In rare moments of leisure time (I was still a busy executive), I began to read about the first few centuries of Christianity. In doing so, I stumbled upon something extraordinary—a direct link between early Christianity and the Catholic Church. As mentioned above, Catholicism was heavily marginalized in the Baptist version of Christian history, and though I was no longer Baptist, my mindset was that Catholicism was still an aberration of the early Church. This link, however, was a novel discovery, and I wanted to learn more.

CHAPTER SEVEN

Common Ground: Baptist and Catholic Beliefs

As I mentioned above, my Father often told me as I was growing up to "step into another person's shoes" to get some sense of their perspective. I had heard many things about how Baptists and Catholics differed, but I wanted to understand also where they had common ground. Though the words "ecumenism" and "ecumenical" were considered dirty in the Baptist vocabulary—because they carried the scent of compromise—I also knew from my Bible that God intended for his people to be unified.

In the Old Testament, we know that the One True God wanted a people to call his own who were separated out of the world and dedicated to him. Adam and Eve messed up, and the earth became so violent that God destroyed it with a flood, saving only one family: Noah's. Almost beginning again with Noah, the world still produced a populace that was in rebellion against their Creator God. By the time God chose Abram, taking him out of Ur (an ancient city in Mesopotamia, now modern Iraq) to build his great nation, the Mesopotamians were worshipping various "gods."

God would indeed create a new Hebrew race from the loins of Abram (later Abraham), but even that new "family" of the one true God was embattled as a human institution and unable to remain unified for any length of time. How often have we read in the histories and chronicles of the Kings where for every good king Hezekiah, there was a wicked king Ahaz. Abraham's family was often a house divided, literally and spiritually. And not only did their family feud internally, but often strayed in worship, choosing gods such as Baal over the God of Israel. In just one of many stories accounted in the Old Testament, we read how God, who only wanted a united people dedicated strictly to him, was either followed or rejected by his own people.

When King Hezekiah came to be ruler over Judah, he re-opened the Temple at Jerusalem that had been plundered and desecrated. He repaired portions of it and had it reconsecrated to God, and, after that, he promulgated a decree that all should come to Jerusalem to keep the Passover of the Lord, the God of Israel. Though many scorned and mocked, having become worshippers of "strange" gods, others came, and we are told that the "power of God was on the people in Judah to give them one heart to obey the command of the king and his officials according to the word of the LORD." Keeping the family of God united, even when tied by blood, was a constant challenge throughout Old Testament history.

Under the Old Covenant (the Law), God in his divine mercy and providence called out the Hebrews as a people separated unto him and him alone. They were not to be separated among themselves, which happened through divisions and in-fighting, but to separate from the world that worshipped other gods. The Hebrews were meant to be a family of believers and the light in the darkness that would foreshadow the light to come in Jesus Christ.

Fast forward just over 700 years from King Hezekiah to the New Testament, and we once again see God creating one family, the Church, made of both Hebrews and Gentiles, who worship the One God. Like the Old Testament, where God created a family bonded by a hereditary bloodline, in the New Testament we also see a bond of blood, but unlike the natural bond of blood among family members, this was a supernatural bond through the blood of our Savior and Lord, Jesus Christ. In Christ, all may become part of God's one family as adopted sons and daughters. And like the Hebrews under the Old Covenant who were separated out as a chosen people by God, so, too, is the Church separated out from the world. For she is not the Body of many gods, but the one body of the one God, whose head (of the body) is Christ.

In looking at both the oneness of God and seeing his desire for one people dedicated unto him throughout history, I could not help but be saddened by the Church's lack of unity. How often has God wanted to wrap his children in his arms only to have them pull away. We see this clearly when, as Jesus is reflecting on Jerusalem not long before his death, he says in Luke 13:34, "Jerusalem, Jerusalem, the city that kills the prophets and stones those who have been sent to her! How often I wanted to gather your children together, just as a hen gathers her young under her wings, and you were unwilling!" And later in Chapter 19:41, we read how Jesus wept over Jerusalem. That the Hebrews had continually divided amongst themselves and willingly refused to follow their God broke our Lord's heart.

Jesus is not with us now physically to show his tears as he most assuredly would weep over the division and strife, rebellion and faction that has damaged his beloved Bride over the many recent centuries. Think about it. With his blood he created a new family of believers to worship the One and Only God, and yet we, his adopted children, those he calls "friends, brothers and mothers," are no better in conduct than the Hebrews of old. Does not our lack of unity alone grieve him? And what of our historical violence, in both word and deed, that Christians have manifested against each other? It is more than a pity; it is an outright shame that those who have been purchased by the blood of the lamb should contest with each other to the extent that the Church has become a house divided and a poor testimony to the world she is here to enlighten.

As I looked into the various Christian churches, I could only see the obvious—that we were all somehow different. In my childhood, I was raised with an emphasis placed on the "difference" between churches and never about what they held in common. Baptists were not interested in understanding where they agreed with another denomination, only on where they disagreed, and this became the focal point and foundation for the separatist mentality.

With a mind more mature now than when I was a child, I took it upon myself to seek out the common ground, choosing that of Baptists and Catholics, both of whom consider themselves Christian but appear to be the furthest apart in a family divided. What I discovered, in the amount of common faith, was significant.

In the table below I summarized the core tenets of the faith that are shared between Baptists and Catholics.

Fundamental Christian Belief	Baptist	Catholic
1 One God in Three Persons	Yes	Yes
2 Worship God Alone	Yes	Yes
3 Virgin Birth of Jesus	Yes	Yes
4 Miracles	Yes	Yes
5 Jesus' Death, Burial & Resurrection	Yes	Yes
6 Atoning Work of Christ	Yes	Yes
7 Baptism in the name of the Father, Son, and Holy Spirit	Yes	Yes
8 Communion/Lord's Supper	Yes	Yes
9 Keeping the 10 Commandments	Yes	Yes
10 God is the Author of Scripture	Yes	Yes
11 Christ the Head/Church the Body	Yes	Yes
12 One Lord, One Faith, One Baptism	Yes	Yes
13 Life after Physical Death	Yes	Yes
14 Eternity in Heaven or Hell	Yes	Yes
15 One Life / After that Judgement	Yes	Yes
16 Second Coming of Jesus Christ	Yes	Yes
17 Belief in Angels/Demons/Satan	Yes	Yes
18 The Great Commandment	Yes	Yes
19 Human Free Will	Yes	Yes
20 Centrality of Love/Charity	Yes	Yes

From this simple list, I concluded that both Baptists and Catholics were Christian and that they agreed on the basic New Testament tenets of the faith. Does that sound strange? It was to me, for in being raised Baptist I was told that, "If a Catholic was a true Christian, it was in spite of the Catholic Church and not because of it." In comparing the common ground, I found it even more difficult to swallow the Baptist and Reformation rhetoric on which I had been raised and began to see that crux of division had to do as much with pride and politics as theological concerns.

The pretentiousness, the jockeying for theological position seen both today and historically, is too easily observable. Individuals filled with righteous smugness took it upon themselves to "correct" errors, real and perceived, by *dismembering* the Body of Christ. Through an unending series of separations, never intended by Christ or the apostles, the Church has become the opposite of Romans 12:16, which states, "Live in harmony with one another. Do not be proud, but enjoy the company of the lowly. Do not be conceited."

We, as the Body of Christ, do not share one mind or voice in glorifying God (Romans 15:6). We, as a Church, are not unified as One Body, in One Spirit, by One Lord, One Faith, and One Baptism (Ephesians 4:4-5). We, as a family of believers, are still infants, "tossed about by the waves and carried around by every wind of teaching and by the clever cunning of men in their deceitful scheming." (Ephesians 4:14)

After two millennia, many followers of Jesus Christ are still overwhelmingly juvenile in the faith—preferring to bicker than share, and hate than love. No Christian of any "label" can ever convince me that this is the will of God.

†††

Regarding separation, which I had previously mentioned as one of the "badges" of merit among Baptists, God has only asked two things from the Church. First, that we separate ourselves from the world; II Cor. 6 states that we are not to be in fellowship with darkness, wickedness, and unbelievers. Second, that we dispel meddlers (heretics) that come into our midst to deny what we know to be truth revealed by God. I can find nowhere in Scripture or Tradition or Early Church History where God welcomes, advocates, or invokes schism among the members of his one family, the Church.

By understanding what Catholics and Baptists held in common belief, and already versed in Baptist, and some Reformed, history, I was compelled to study beyond my personal research. The need was ever-present to understand, at the deepest level, whether or not the New Testament Church was originally Catholic. It was time to step into the shoes of this 2,000-year-old Church and see what it was made of. With that goal in mind, I was able to find one school that offered a graduate degree in Theology with a concentration in Church History. That was exactly what I was looking for, and I applied.

CHAPTER EIGHT

Shadows Dispelling,
with Joy I am Telling

To say that I was enthusiastic to begin my coursework would be an understatement. I was thrilled. A geek at heart, I was excited to delve into the rich pool of knowledge that had escaped me as a youth. For the first time, I would study the history of Christianity from the time of the Apostles to the Reformation and post-Reformation period, and I looked forward to every single class.

Beginning with Koine Greek, the primary language of the New Testament, followed by courses in Theology and Church history, I started a five-year journey to understand the early formation of the Church, her doctrinal developments, and her many struggles. As the years progressed, I gained an appreciation for the Catholic contribution to Church history, particularly in doctrinal development which was often, more than not, a refutation of false teachings that plagued the Church in the first few centuries. The shadows of my Baptist youth, which had shrouded Catholicism in a mist of degrading propaganda, began to dispel as I learned that the post-apostolic Church was actually *Catholic*. That I had reached this conclusion was alone worth my time and money, but it wasn't the only benefit.

Unlike my Baptist college days where questions were often suspect, I now found myself in an academic arena where inquiries were encouraged. And not only that, but questions were an integral part of the learning process. Even questions from an Evangelical Christian student were not considered stupid! When I raised my internet hand, not a single professor replied, "Well, that is what the Church teaches." It was a refreshing experience to learn in an environment without intimidation.

†††

Studying with classmates from around the globe, we delved into the "why, what, and how" of ecclesial and doctrinal development. Our readings, taken from early pastoral and apologetical works, were all foreign to me. My fellow-students, most, if not all being Catholic, had some inkling of the authors we read and discussed, while I had no clue who Irenaeus or Athanasius were. It was a new perspective as we immersed ourselves in a reservoir of Church history and literature. One would need to take the courses to grasp the depth of learning, but what impressed me the most was the continual thread of fidelity woven through those early centuries. It was clear that the infant Church had been gifted by the Holy Spirit with leaders devoted to preserving the New Testament faith. Their loyalty to Christ and the teachings of the apostles was reflected in their work, lives, and for some, even death as martyrs.

Reading histories, including primary sources, it became clear that in the years immediately succeeding the apostles, the Church was confronted with heretical teachings—teachings in contradiction to established orthodoxy. At the gate of the sheepfold, there was inevitably a person or group that wanted to distort, dilute, or dismiss Scripture and apostolic teaching. One such group were called "Gnostics," loosely translated as "Knowers," often priding themselves on their glut of knowledge.

Gnostics were basically spiritual know-it-alls with mixed philosophical and religious views and an appetite for meddling. Considering themselves to be Christian, because they adhered to some tenets of the faith, Gnosticism posed a problem for the early Church as they attempted to introduce views that conflicted with traditional teaching. Not long after the death of the apostles, a Gnostic named Marcion (ca. 85-160 A.D.), who described himself as a "Christian Gnostic," began to preach that God was not one, but two persons. His two-part god, a direct contradiction to the monotheistic nature of God, was called "dualism," and it consisted of an "evil" God of the Old Testament, and a "loving" God of the New Testament. In addition to this heretical teaching, Marcion also did not accept the divinity of Jesus Christ, because no perfect God would condescend to the world of human flesh—matter being considered evil.

By reading about the lives and works of the early Church fathers and their various struggles, I was able to grasp not only the "what" of doctrine—the final product we are most familiar with—but also *how* and *why* doctrines came into existence. It became evident that in studying the first four hundred years of the Church, a constant vigil was kept against error to ensure the trustworthiness of the apostolic faith.

†††

Among the many challenges the Church faced, there was one heretical teaching in particular that cemented my appreciation for the Catholic development of Christian doctrine. This controversial heresy, which has been called both a "question" and a "problem," was an attack on the established Church teaching of the Holy Trinity—One God in Three Persons.

As the apostles of Christ spread the gospel geographically, with no small help from the apostle Paul's three missionary journeys, churches could be found spanning the entire region around the Mediterranean sea. After the death of Paul and the other apostles, the Church continued to spread the gospel inland and to North of Africa. Around 300 A.D., some converts in the East, many from monotheistic Judaism or polytheistic paganism, became suspicious of the teaching on the Holy Trinity, and a debate on the nature of God ensued. The nature of God became a hot topic that spread quickly among the churches from North Africa to Syria. As speculation increased, so too did erroneous proposals, including one that denied the Trinity existed. The magnitude of this controversy would have a lasting impact on the universal Church such that it is impossible for me to not insert a *little* Church history into my conversion story. For it was studying the historical component of doctrinal development that entirely altered my perspective on Catholicism.

CHAPTER NINE

A "Little" Church History

During the first centuries after Christs' accension, the Church was scattered geographically, outnumbered by non-Christians, and illegal in the Roman Empire. These three factors, whether separate or combined, enabled the proliferation of speculation and subsequent heretical teachings that were easily fostered in the darkness of forced secret worship. If your religion is illegal, it is difficult to communicate outside your circle, let alone publicly debate aspects of the faith. When the ban on Christianity was lifted in 313 A.D. by the Edict of Milan, these erroneous teachings erupted into the open and like a wild wind from every direction, the Church was now publicly battered by false teachers who threw everything at her to see if it would stick. It also did not help that many doctrines we take for granted today were not "ready-made" in the early Church, for words such as "Trinity" and "Incarnate" are not found in Scripture.

Belief in One God in Three Persons, however, had been a core tenet of faith since the time of the apostles and is clearly seen in the rite of Baptism when it is proclaimed in "The name of the Father, and of the Son, and of the Holy Spirit" (Matthew 28:19). Yet, the concept of a Trinity, the math behind 1 and 3, was a stumbling block for some believers who associated it with polytheism. Not only was this a logical observation, but the Judaic roots of monotheism were embedded in and still maintained within Christianity. That God is One was clear, but the idea of One God who is also Triune was bewildering, and the issue stirred up no small debate, with churches taking up sides as either pro-Trinitarian or non-Trinitarian.

Though the nature of God is a mystery believed, the early fathers found themselves compelled to answer the question, "How can this be?" in order to maintain the integrity of the Trinity. Attempting to define a mystery in human terms would be no small feat, but in light of a growing error, called Arianism, it would have to be done.

†††

One of the most influential of speculative, yet flawed teachers to rise after the legalization of Christianity was Arius of Alexandria (ca. 270-336 A.D.). The initial focus of the Trinitarian debate was centered on the divinity of Jesus

Christ. To maintain the unquestionable monotheistic nature of God, Arius, a deacon and later priest in Alexandria, was convinced that there was no Trinity. At a time when oration and rhetoric were often prized for their style over content, Arius eloquently asserted that Jesus was the only begotten *human* son of God—a unique creature elevated to divinity by God, but a creature, nonetheless. This proposal, which sounds absurd to the Church today, appeared reasonable to those dedicated to the monotheistic nature of God. While still holding Jesus Christ in esteem as Savior, Arius' proposal was convincing, and he accumulated many followers including some Eastern bishops and priests. As his confidence and clerical support swelled, he would ultimately defend his position openly to his Bishop, Alexander of Alexandria, by writing, "*We acknowledge one God, alone unbegotten...who begot an only-begotten Son...a perfect creature of God. (ca. 320 A.D.)*[5]

Arius' answer to the Trinitarian question of "How can this be" was to reply, it cannot be. Jesus was *made* a divine person, an important factor in the economy of salvation, but he was neither co-equal nor co-eternal with God the

[5] Jurgens, W.A., trans. And ed. *The Faith of the Early Fathers, Vol. I.* (Collegeville: The Liturgical Press 1970). p. 277.

Father. Now Bishop Alexander, a staunch Trinitarian, was neither impressed nor surprised by the letter, having previously excommunicated Arius at the regional Council of Egypt in 318 A.D., but the fact that Arius was publicly pronouncing his argument two years later indicated that the threat of Arianism was gaining momentum within the newly legalized Church.

The argument of Arius is more complicated than what I have briefly presented, but the point is that his ability to articulate a case against the Trinity was too easily accepted. His temporary success was due in part because error was able to fester in the darkness where for over a century Christians were forced to practice and for some speculate, in secret, and in part because there had been no universal and authoritative definition to explain the Trinity. In the absence of a definitive doctrine, Arius' teaching against the Trinity nearly engulfed the Eastern Church. As Jerome (ca. 347-420 A.D.), the great theologian, historian, and Latin translator of the Vulgate Bible, reflected on this in his work *Dialogue between a Luciferian and an Orthodox Christian* (379 A.D.), "The whole world groaned when, to its astonishment, it discovered that it was Arian."

To combat this invasive heresy, which quite literally would have altered the Christian faith to the extent that it would be unrecognizable to the apostles, another council was called, but this time it would be ecumenical. The council of Egypt in 318 A.D. had been regional, but with the spread of Arianism in the East, a Church-wide council was needed, and not only to dispel the theological error. While Arianism was a doctrinal threat to the Church, it had become a political issue as well. So political that in 325 A.D. the Roman Emperor Constantine, who had legalized Christianity in 313 A.D., took the lead in calling the council. He was an unhappy politician who witnessed the Christological dispute not only divide the newly recognized Church, but saw it spill over into the public streets. Whether Jesus Christ, the Son of God, was equal (or not) to God the Father, incited brawls between opposing parties, monks as well as lay persons. What had begun as a theological controversy among the clergy was now disrupting Constantine's newly achieved *Pax Romana,* and it had to be stopped. To settle the matter, the Emperor called an ecumenical council at Nicaea, a city near his home in Constantinople, the new capital city of the empire.

Over 300 bishops of the church, primarily Eastern, attended the council that lasted for just under three months.[6] Among the attendees was Alexander, with his deacon and

---

[6] There had been a few Westerners present, but the Trinitarian debate was primarily contested in the East where Arianism had flourished.

future successor, Athanasius. Arius and his supporters
were also present. By the end of the council, the teachings
of Arius were formally condemned and officially refuted in
the writing and adoption of the Nicene Creed in 325 A.D.
This creed ("creed" is from the Latin *credo* for "I believe")
would summarize for the benefit of all what the Church
had always believed—that Jesus Christ, the Son of God, is
consubstantial with the Father.[7] The Creed, which begins
with One God, further defines the nature of the Trinity by
clarifying (italicized below) the position of Jesus Christ in
a specific rebuttal of Arius' teaching:

> I believe in one God, the Father almighty,
> maker of heaven and earth, of all things vis-
> ible and invisible.

> I believe in one Lord Jesus Christ, the Only
> Begotten Son of God, *born of the Father be-*
> *fore all ages. God from God, Light from*
> *Light, true God from true God, begotten, not*
> *made, consubstantial with the Father...*

---

[7] The issue of the Trinity was highly complex. Here, I some-
what oversimplified both the Christological and Pneumatological aspects of the debate. It is well worth it to study the history
of the Nicene Creed.

The Christological controversy, the result of heterodox teaching, gifted the Church with The Nicene Creed—a universal and definitive summary of core Christian tenets surrounding the Trinity. Yet the struggle was not over, for in the decades that followed the council of Nicaea, the Arians continued their rejection of the Trinity, and soon others began a similar attack against the 3rd Person of the Trinity, the Holy Spirit. With the Pneumatological controversy, the Catholic camp was once again divided and as each group vied for control, excommunications and forced resignations became weapons of regional warfare. Nicaea had won a significant battle, turning the tide of war in favor of the Trinity, but ultimate victory remained elusive until the Holy Spirit blessed the Church with two spiritual generals.

As ardent defenders of the Nicene Creed: Athanasius, Bishop of Alexandria (d. 373 A.D.), who had attended Nicaea as a deacon to Bishop Alexander, and his Western counterpart, Hilary of Poitiers, Bishop of Lyons (d. 367/8 A.D.) would bring the war to a close. This spiritual duo continued the struggle for the Trinity through homilies, letters, and treatises sent to friends, foes, and fence straddlers. It was a battle royal, but when it was over, the Trinitarians had won, with the Nicene Creed reaffirmed at the Council of Constantinople in 381 A.D., with the following language (italicized below) added regarding the Holy Spirit[8].

> And in the Holy Spirit, *the Lord and Giver of life, who proceeds from the Father, who with the Father and the Son together is worshiped and glorified, who spoke by the prophets.*

The Trinitarian controversy that had begun over One God in Three Persons had spanned more than 60 years before it finally came to an end with the framing of a crystal-clear doctrine. The codification of this doctrine came as a result of errors introduced into the newly legalized Church and early fathers willing and able to step up and defend the traditional truths by providing clear definitions.

†††

It is easy to take for granted the challenges of the early Church; 20/20 hindsight and the modern mentality often devalue historical accomplishments. Yet if history is stu-

---

[8] A full side-by-side comparison of the two Creeds may be found in the appendix.

died within the context of the time, it can provide priceless insight. It had that impact on me.

Like the not-ready-for-prime-time doctrinal definitions, the Bible itself, and as we know it today, had not been compiled during Arius' life. The complete Old Testament had been in existence during the time of Christ, but the New Testament was not assembled until the 4th century. At the request of Pope Damasus I, who called a council in 382 A.D. in Rome, and under the guidance of the Holy Spirit, the twenty-seven books of the New Testament were canonized. But even if the New Testament had been complete and in possession at every church from Rome to Carthage, it did not contain defined doctrines. Under the continued guidance of the Holy Spirit, the Councils of Nicaea and Constantinople played crucial roles in clarifying and summarizing extant truths into a single Creed. The importance of this Creed should not be undermined, for in being succinct, it was more than a summation; it was a tool for evangelization and discipleship. At a time when there was no printing press, or individually owned Bibles, the Creed offered a way to memorize major tenets of the faith, and in doing so, truly write the Gospel on the hearts of Christians everywhere.

CHAPTER TEN

Wondering, "Am I Catholic?"

About three years into my theological training and a full ten years after returning to Christianity, it occurred to me that I might be Catholic. It was just a thought. I had only been to one Mass, and that was with a Catholic aunt, unless funerals and weddings count, then three more times. Whatever the number, the point is that I had minimal in-person exposure to Catholicism; everything I had learned thus far had been focused on history and theology in an academic setting. Yet, there was another face of Catholicism that needed to be examined, and as I pondered my potential "catholicity," I could no longer avoid the elephant in the cathedral: the recent sex abuse scandals that had rocked America and the world.

From the perspective of a life-long outsider, I had come to view the Catholic Church as paradoxically beautiful and ugly. As an historically utilitarian Christian, whose worship experience was bare-boned, the external beauty of the Catholic Church—reflected in ornate architecture, magnificent stained-glass windows, and Gregorian music—

was indeed lovely. As a globe-trotter, I had been impressed by her many cathedrals, including Saints Peter and Paul's in Rome as well as her collection of artistic masterpieces. She was culturally and physically beautiful to look upon. Yet, at the same time, on an institutional level, I also found her to be a white-washed sepulcher as news of the ugly sex abuse scandals filled the national and global airwaves for years on end.

As a Christian, it was impossible for me to turn a blind eye to proven acts of vile behavior against humanity, and the almost daily revelations of abuse at this or that Catholic Diocese sickened me. Something so vulgar could not be easily swept aside, and if I were to seriously consider conversion, I would have to address this issue.

†††

Only a person who lived in a cave could claim ignorance regarding the increasingly wide-spread national and global abuse scandals that have surfaced in the past thirty years. And the magnitude of abuse at the institutional level, being high profile, is but the tip of an endemic abuse iceberg mostly hidden from view. Americans watched in horror as the Boy Scouts of America disintegrated with thousands of

Scouts revealing sexual abuse by their leaders. And when the news broke about the USA Gymnastics abuse scandal, where minors had been subjected to unconscionable acts by coaching staff and their team physician, we were again appalled. Institutions meant to build up our youth were damaging them one by one, and in the midst of it all was the Roman Catholic Church.

As for myself, I have never been abused, but I cannot help but get angry at the idea of an adult preying on another, let alone a child; and I knew that Jesus felt the same way. To break a sacred trust and dishonor God by harming another person, particularly a little one, Jesus referenced in Matthew 18:4-7:

> Whoever humbles himself and becomes like this child is the greatest in the kingdom of heaven. And whoever receives one such child in my name receives me. But if anyone causes one of these little ones who believe in me to sin, it would be better for him to have a millstone fastened around his neck and to be drowned in the depths of the sea. Woe to the world because of scandals. Such things are bound to occur, but woe to the one through whom they come.

God has the highest standards of human conduct, and he made himself very clear in Scripture, where even a thought is considered sin no less grave than an action (Gen. 6:5, Matt. 5:28, Mark 7:21).

That the earthly Body of Christ consists of flawed individuals bent toward sin is no surprise. We are regenerated, that is to say, reconciled to God as a new creature in Christ. But this does not eliminate the old nature; we remain capable of sin. That Christ and his Body are marred by harmful conduct is utterly unacceptable and a disgrace above the magnitude of any earthly institution. That being understood, how could I ever consider conversion knowing the high-profile scandal associated with Roman Catholicism?[9] This was not an easy question to answer. Again, I had to pray, and, in doing so, I was forced to look at myself and the person of Jesus Christ.

My nature is capable of any sin that another human is capable of, and to say otherwise is a lie. We often hear about the shock of others who, upon finding that a relative or neighbor committed "this or that" violent act, recoil in

---

[9] Other Christian denominations, including recent revelations regarding the Southern Baptist Convention, are culpable of abuse as well. The Roman Catholic Church, however, being a globally high-profile and centralized institution, required non-theological self-reflection on my part.

disbelief and retort, "They could never have done that terrible deed!" But people of all backgrounds do terrible things, and to deny this is to ignore the reality of our sinful nature. In becoming a new creature, my standard of conduct was raised to an even higher setting than that of the world, but the bottom still remained.

In understanding my nature, both old and new, and what was expected of me, I was compelled to shift my focus to Jesus Christ. The Church, which includes me, is composed of imperfect humans subject to sin, yet the head, Jesus Christ, is perfect and sinless. It is my sin that directly reflects upon him and the Church. The apostle Paul wanted us to imitate Christ, not only for our own good, but for the good of the Church and Christ himself. Jesus cannot damage the reputation of the Church, but the Church can damage Jesus' reputation. This can be seen clearly in the saying of Mahatma Gandhi who once stated, "I like your Christ. I do not like your Christians. Your Christians are so unlike your Christ."

By acknowledging and not excusing my human nature, and by looking to the perfect nature of Christ, I was able to understand that if I look to myself or other humans, I will inevitably be disappointed when I, or they, fail to live up to Christs' perfect standard. The sin of a Christian is not committed in a void; it impacts others as well as ourselves and therein lies the fragile nature of rebirth. But we do not need to be fragile, for we are encouraged to mature and in so doing imitate the one "who knew no sin." Perhaps, then, more people will witness Christians as they were perceived, and named, at Antioch.

†††

When something ugly happens in the world or within the context of the Church, the only way I am able to survive is to remain focused on Jesus, the perfector of our faith. If I had only considered the Catholic Church's physical beauty, or ugly revelations, Roman Catholicism would have been little more than a blip on my radar. But I knew that from a strictly human standpoint, I had to keep my eyes on Jesus. Convicted of this, I was able to not ignore, but acknowledge the elephant in the cathedral, and freely return to the idea of becoming aligned with the Catholic Church. The next step would be to address other issues embedded in my cradle Baptist brain: the negative propaganda I had heard all my life about the Roman Catholic Church.

†††

Bigotry and myth, whether political, cultural, or religious, are ideological ammunition used by manipulative persons to, hopefully, persuade a populace through deceit. These people utilize a tool called propaganda, which normally carries a negative context but is really just a form of advertising or marketing. Whether the motive be true or false, the point of propaganda is to compel a person to act before they think, hoping that an emotional decision will benefit their immediate cause. It could be as simple as buying that new car "you deserve" to degrading a whole populace for political support. This last example is best seen in the work of Nazi Chief Propagandist Joseph Goebbels whose only goal was to elevate the German Aryan ideal above all other peoples; and we all know how that ended. Not unlike advertising, propaganda with the right psychological emphasis and slick marketing skills can cloak fiction as fact; and it was my responsibility to separate the two by starting with the person of Mary.

††††

The person and role of Mary, the mother of Jesus, is particularly divisive among modern Catholic and Protestant Christians. Many 16th-century Reformers believed that there was "too much ado" about Mary, often condemning Catholics of idolatry. With the advent of the printing press in 1450, both religious and political anti-Catholic propaganda could be easily disseminated among the populace. Though the populations of Europe and England were largely illiterate, most adults could understand printed satire, such as depicting the Pope as the devil in elaborate cartoons. And in England, the mother of America, anti-Catholicism was all the rage.

In England, where Henry VIII had desecrated and plundered monastic possessions and land (1536-1541 A.D.) to fill his pockets and those of his newly formed Church of England, and where, later, his daughter Queen Elizabeth I would legally impose the Church of England on her citizens (1559 Act of Uniformity), anything that remotely hinted of the Catholic religion was driven underground. This suppression of Catholics, as well as non-conforming Protestants, lasted for 200 years, and though these actions were both politically and religiously motivated to unify and stabilize England, anti-Catholic sentiment carried across the pond to the new American colonies and continued to prevail up to recent times. What I wanted to know was, since the Reformation idea of Catholics worshipping Mary still persists today in America, is it a fact or is it fiction?

It did not take me that long to conclude that Catholics do not worship Mary. And not only that, but just like Henry's Church of England, Catholics reserve worship to God alone. The idolizing of Mary was a myth.

Technically speaking, Catholics "venerate" Mary, and while the word "venerate" may have the dictionary definition of *worship, honor, reverence,* or *adoration*, Catholic teaching applies the word strictly as honor and *not* worship. The meaning is similarly expressed in Ephesians 6:2 where Paul declares "*Honor* your father and mother." The word for "honor" comes from the Greek word *Tima* (Τιμα), which may mean, *honor, worship,* or *adoration*, depending on the context. In the context of our parents, we are to honor them, but with God, and him alone, are we to worship. And so it is with Mary, who is not worshipped, but honored by Catholics for her uniquely blessed role in the salvific story. The official teaching of the Catholic Church on Mary, and regarding her veneration, is stated in an excerpt below from the Catechism of the Catholic Church (970-971):

> No creature could ever be counted along with the Incarnate Word and Redeemer. Devotion to the Blessed Virgin differs essentially from the adoration which is given

to the Incarnate Word and equally to the
Father and the Holy Spirit.

Research based on evidence, such as in the case of Mary,
allowed me to clear up many myths generated by historical
propaganda and helped me to narrow the list of crucial
theological differences between Catholics and Baptists.
That final list, which would determine whether my journey
to Catholicism would succeed or fail, was composed of six
doctrines at the crux of historical disputation.

CHAPTER ELEVEN

The Big Six

As years of formal theological training came to a close, I concluded that the most significant differences between Baptist and Catholic theology center on six doctrinal teachings. All six were prominent issues during the Reformation and remain a formidable *crevasse* for Baptists today. The first two, Apostolic Succession and the Primacy of Peter, deal with the Church's ecclesial structure. The third regards the role of Tradition, and the fourth and fifth, both closely tied together, deal with the Eucharist (aka Lord's Supper, Holy Communion) and the idea of Christ being re-sacrificed at Mass. The final regards Baptism.

Apostolic Succession.

Apostolic succession is the unbroken line of Catholic bishops traced back to the time of the Apostles. It is a chief component of the unified and organic structure of the Church.

The Church, defined by Paul in Ephesians 2:20, was founded upon the Apostles and Prophets, with Jesus Christ as the chief corner stone. It was the foundation for a living, universal, and Christ-minded body of believers. The Church is like a house that is to be continually built until Christ comes again. Irenaeus, the second Bishop of Lyons, in his work *Against Heresies* (ca. 180 A.D.) wrote:

> As I said before, the Church, having received this preaching and this faith, although she is disseminated throughout the whole world, yet guarded it, as if she occupied but one house.

Apostolic succession is an integral part of the continual building of the one house, to fulfill the command of Matthew 28:19-20:

> Go, therefore, and make disciples of all nations, baptizing them in the name of the Father, and of the Son, and of the holy Spirit, teaching them to observe all that I have commanded you. And behold, I am with you always, until the end of the age.

To comply with the Lord's command, and maintain the unity of the faith, the apostles appointed successor bishops who would continue construction after their deaths. It was a hierarchy based in Scripture that included bishops (I Tim. 3:1; Titus 1:7), presbyters (I Tim. 4:14), and deacons (Acts 6; Phil. 1:1; I Tim. 3:8).

The oral and written methods employed by the apostles enabled a seamless transmission of authoritative teaching to the next generation of shepherds. The apostolic fathers—those who either knew or lived during the time of the apostles—understood their grave responsibility. Consider the following passage by Ignatius, the 3rd Bishop of Antioch (Peter being the first), in his *Letter to the Ephesians* (ca. 110 A.D.):

> For Jesus Christ, our inseparable life, is the will of the Father, just as the bishops who have been appointed throughout the world, are the will of Jesus Christ.[10]

---

[10] Jurgens, W.A., trans. And ed. *The Faith of the Early Fathers, Vol. I.* (Collegeville: The Liturgical Press, 1970), p. 17.

The Church, is a hierarchy that begins with the monarch, Jesus Christ, who appointed, with authority, the twelve apostles. The apostles carried on this tradition by appointing "overseers" from the Greek *episkopon,* which is translated into English as "bishop." Since then, the role of Catholic bishop, the pastor of a local flock of churches called a diocese, is appointed by the Church. Unlike an independent Evangelical Pastor, a Catholic Bishop is not the sole authority on faith and morals for his churches. He cannot simply go out and start his own church and teach whatever he wants because his authority is subject to the Church. In this way, the universal body remains one and faithful to Christ and the apostles.

Apostolic succession is the divinely appointed structure of the Church, guided by the Holy Spirit to ensure that future generations have access to the original truths of the early Church.

Baptists do not believe in apostolic succession. The Church of England does recognize apostolic succession, however their split from the Catholic Church broke apostolic unity.

Primacy of Peter

The primacy or "chair" of Peter refers to the role of the bishop of Rome as the "bishop of bishops." Like apostolic succession, it is a unique position of leadership within the hierarchal structure of the Church and can be traced back in both Scripture and early tradition.

When Jesus gave his command to the twelve apostles, he also focused on the role that Peter would play. In the Gospel of Matthew, when Jesus asks, "Who do men say that I am?" we read Peter's confession, and our Lords response:

> He said to them, "But who do you say that I am?" Simon Peter said in reply, "You are the Messiah, the Son of the living God." Jesus said to him in reply, "Blessed are you, Simon son of Jonah. For flesh and blood has not revealed this to you, but my heavenly Father. And so I say to you, you are Peter, and upon this rock I will build my church, and the gates of the netherworld shall not prevail against it. I will give you the keys to the kingdom of heaven. Whatever you bind on earth shall be bound in heaven; and

whatever you loose on earth shall be loosed
in heaven. (Matthew 16:15-19)

One thing stood out to me as I reviewed the meaning of "I
will give you the keys to the kingdom of heaven." Peter was
essentially becoming a "gatekeeper," which was not always a
position of honor (as with the Levites in the Temple). At the
time of Christ, a wealthy household—Roman or otherwise—
would have slaves in attendance. Among those who served
the master of the house, was a door or gate keeper who was
responsible for managing traffic in and out, as well as secur-
ing the door. It was considered to be one of the lowest positions in the master's house, though one of the most responsible.

In the Gospel of John, we find the resurrected Jesus
speaking to Peter, with Peter's three denials of Christ still
fresh in both their minds:

> When they had finished breakfast, Jesus
> said to Simon Peter, "Simon, son of John,
> do you love me more than these?" He said
> to him, "Yes, Lord, you know that I love
> you." He said to him, "Feed my lambs." He
> then said to him a second time, "Simon, son
> of John, do you love me?" He said to him,

"Yes, Lord, you know that I love you." He
said to him, "Tend my sheep." He said to
him the third time, "Simon, son of John, do
you love me?" Peter was distressed that he
had said to him a third time, "Do you love
me?" and he said to him, "Lord, you know
everything; you know that I love you." [Jesus] said to him, "Feed my sheep." (John
21:15-17)

Similar to the lowly, yet responsible, position of gate
keeper, Christ is here admonishing Peter to be a shepherd.
During biblical times, a shepherd garnered little respect yet
was imputed with a grave responsibility. He was the person
to tend the master's flock, feeding them and keeping them
safe, often at his own peril. It was no luxury to sleep in the
gate of a fold, with only the moon and stars for company.
The role that Peter would play is truly paradoxical, for it is
both lowly in rank, but elevated in responsibility.

In addition to Scripture, the special role that Peter, and
his bishop successors, would play is implicitly and explicitly recorded in early Church History.

Clement, Bishop of Rome

Around 80 A.D., the church at Corinth had written to Clement asking for guidance. We do not have their letter, but we have Clement's reply, part of which includes the following:

> Owing to the sudden and repeated calamities and misfortunes which have befallen us, we must acknowledge that we have been somewhat tardy in turning our attention to the matters in dispute among you, beloved; and especially that abominable and unholy sedition, alien and foreign to the elect of God, which a few rash and self-willed persons have inflamed to such madness that your venerable and illustrious name, worthy to be loved by all men, has been greatly defamed.[11]

When the church at Corinth (in modern Greece) had an issue, they looked to the Bishop of Rome for answers, and

---

[11] Jurgens, W.A., trans. and ed. *The Faith of the Early Fathers, Vol. I.* (Collegeville: The Liturgical Press, 1970), p. 7.

Clement was not surprised by this fact, but replied with presumed duty and authority. For the church at Corinth, whose "founding father" Paul was with Christ in heaven, it seemed natural to subordinate themselves to the successor of Peter (and Paul); the current Roman Bishop.[12]

Cyprian, Bishop of Carthage

In the first edition of his treatise,[13] on *The Unity of the Catholic Church*, (ca. 250 A.D.), Cyprian, who resided in what is now modern Tunisa, recognized the leadership of the Bishop of Rome.

> The Lord says to Peter: "I say to you," He says, "that you are Peter, and upon this rock I will build my Church, and the gates of hell will not overcome it."

---

[12] It is interesting to note that the Papacy utilizes PP in their insignia, representing both Peter and Paul.

[13] It would be remiss of me to not address that in the second edition, four years later, Cyprian dilutes some of his pro-Rome language. The editing appears to have appeased some otherwise upset Bishops who did not yet recognize Papal Primacy on a *universal* level. His first letter is, however, an implicit example of doctrine-under-development.

And again, He says to him after his resurrection: "Feed my sheep." On him He builds the Church, and to him He gives the command to feed the sheep; and although He assigns a like power to all the Apostles, yet he founded a single chair, and He established by His own authority a source and an intrinsic reason for that unity. Indeed, the other were that also which Peter was; but a primacy is given to Peter, whereby it is made clear that there is but one Church and one chair.[14]

†††

Within independent Baptist churches, the Primacy of Peter is a fabrication of the Catholic Church. I recall hearing many times that Jesus had made a "play on words" and meant that he, [Jesus], was the intended "rock" while Peter was just a "stone." This argument against Peter's role is directly stated in the *Scofield Reference Bible*, by C.I. Scofield

---

[14] Jurgens, W.A., trans. And ed. *The Faith of the Early Fathers, Vol. I.* (Collegeville: The Liturgical Press, 1970), p. 220.

in his notes on the passage. Regarding Matthew 16:18, Scofield states,

> In the Greek there is a play upon words in this statement: "Thou art Peter [*petros*, a stone], and upon this rock [*petra*, a massive rock] I will build my church.[15]

This play on words is an untenable theory to me because it cannot succeed without manipulating the Greek.

The words for "rock," which Jesus uses in Matthew's gospel, are the Greek words *petros*, (πέτρος), and *petra* (πέτρα), the first being masculine and the second feminine. Both may be used as nouns, such as a physical rock, or transliterated as "Peter," and "Petrina or Petra," as proper names in English. Either of these may mean rock, stone, or boulder. Likewise in John 1:42, we see where Jesus named Peter *Cephas* (Κηφᾶς), an Aramaic term kēpā (כֵּיפָא) that means rock. There is nothing here to substantiate a *stone* versus a *massive rock*. In fact, a common term for "stone" in Scripture is *lithos* (λίθος), most notably used in the "stoning" of Stephen in Acts Chapter 7.

[15] Scofield, C.I., ed. T*he Scofield Reference Bible*, King James Version (Oxford: Oxford University Press, 1907).

As every Christian knows, or should know, the apostle Paul declares that our foundation is built upon the apostles and the prophets with Christ as the chief corner *stone* (Eph. 2:20). That Jesus was playing with words is absurd to me; he knew exactly what he was saying. The time was quickly approaching when he would ascend into heaven and that, in his physical absence, leaders, and a leader among leaders, would be required to build the Church on earth. The investment of an authoritative hierarchy was not seen as a ranking position of status but a structure to safeguard the new Body of Christ. It is not a new concept created by Catholics.

In real life, both in biblical times and today, everywhere we look there is order based upon a hierarchy with one person at the top. Countries have Presidents, Prime Ministers, Kings, and Queens. There are Battalion Chiefs, Police Commissioners, Corporate Presidents, School Principals, Construction Foremen, and a Parent as head of their family. Authoritative hierarchy was given by God to humanity from the very beginning. It makes no sense that our monarchial God would alter the structure and building of his divine House by allowing a plethora of independent contractors to do whatever they wanted. There is One God, one faith, one Bible, and one blueprint for building his Church.

> *Most Baptists do not recognize the biblical roles of Bishop, Presbyter, and Deacon within their own denominations. None recognize the leadership role of Peter as Bishop of Bishops and consequently deny the authority of the Papacy.*

Tradition

Sacred Scripture was written by men, inspired by the Holy Spirit. In the Old Testament, there are works by prophets, priests, and kings spanning a thousand years. In the New Testament, the authors either directly knew Jesus, for example, the apostle John, or closely followed an apostle's testimony and committed it to writing, such as Mark on behalf of Peter.[16] The whole New Testament was written within a few decades after Jesus' ascension.

From the beginning, and prior to the writing and compilation of the New Testament, there was Sacred Tradition—the oral teachings and examples of the Apostles handed down to next generation believers. Sacred Scripture confirms that before there was anything written, the

---

[16] Neither Mark, nor Luke, personally knew Jesus, even though their combined works make up most of the words in the New Testament. They were disciples of Peter and Paul, and their writings, guided by the Holy Spirit, transmitted by written word what they had learned from the apostles orally.

gospel was preached and exemplified by the Apostles and their co-workers. The importance of oral and exemplary tradition was made clear to me when I considered two things, both witnessed by Scripture. First, the exhortations of the Apostles to continue what the recipient of the writing had orally received. Second, the apostolic intent behind the writing. Below are three examples, words in bold are my emphasis:

In his letter to the Philippians (ca. 60 A.D.), a church Paul had founded several years earlier on his second missionary journey, he later wrote to them:

Keep on doing what you have **learned and received and heard and seen** in me. (Philippians 4:9)

Paul's intention in writing the letter was to both thank them and exhort this church to continue in what they had already been taught through his preaching and by his example.

In his letter to the Colossians (ca. 60 A.D.), a church Paul had not visited and was likely founded by one of Paul's converts, Epaphras, he wrote:

...because of the hope reserved for you in heaven. Of this you **have already heard** through the word of truth, the gospel, that has come to you. Just as in the whole world it is bearing fruit and growing, so also among you, **from the day you heard it** and came to know the grace of God in truth, as **you learned it from Epaphras** our beloved fellow slave, who is a trustworthy minister of Christ on your behalf and who also told us of your love in the Spirit. (Colossians 1:5-7)

Paul's intention in writing this letter was to reinforce truths already heard second-hand, so to speak. It had come to his attention that there were strangers in their midst who, with enticing words, spoke things not of Christ.

In his letter to the Galatians (ca. 49 A.D.), a church Paul had visited on both his first and third missionary journeys, he wrote:

I am amazed that you are so quickly forsaking the one who called you by [the] grace [of Christ] for a different gospel (not that there is another). But there are some who are disturbing you and wish to pervert the gospel of Christ. But even if we or an angel from heaven should preach [to you] a gospel other than the one that **we preached to you**, let that one be accursed! **As we have said before**, and now I say again, if anyone preaches to you a gospel other than the one that you received, let that one be accursed! (Galatians 1:6 -9)

Paul's intention in writing this letter was to warn the churches in Galatia about false teachings that threatened previously preached doctrinal purity and purity of conduct.

There are many more examples, these are but a few. What became clear to me was that the tradition of oral teaching, in evangelization and the founding of churches, preceded the writings of the New Testament by years and sometimes decades.

The intentions of the New Testament writers vary from correction to exhortation to instruction, of which all are profitable to us today (II Tim. 3:16). Some books are personally addressed, such as the gospel of Luke written to Theophilus. Others were generally addressed, such as Peter's first letter, written to Hebrew Christians "scattered throughout Pontus, Galatia, Cappadocia, Asia, and Bithynia." And we know that there were other apostolic letters that were written that have not survived to this day.[17]

†††

Throughout my study of Sacred Scripture and Tradition, I often wondered why Jesus passed on his teaching orally to his Apostles instead of having a scribe write down his words and deeds as they happened. It was not uncommon for a religious figure to write their own works. Yet with Jesus, we have nothing in his own hand. Only in one instance, (John 8:6), do we hear of Jesus' scribbling in the sand. What little he did write remains a mystery.

What we do know is that Jesus' life, death, resurrection, teachings, and miracles were seen and heard by the apostles, and many more besides, and that those same apostles verbally transmitted what they saw and heard. Preaching was the *modus operandi* for establishing churches and fulfilling Jesus' command (Matthew 28:18-20). Regarding

---

[17] At the time Paul was writing to the church at Colossae, he asked them to send a copy to the church at Laodicea and to read the epistle from Laodicea; to trade apostolic letters, the latter of which we do not have record of.

Tradition, The *Catechism of the Catholic Church*[18] states (77,78):

> In order that the full and living Gospel might always be preserved in the Church the apostles left bishops as their successors... This living transmission, accomplished in the Holy Spirit, is called Tradition, since it is distinct from Sacred Scripture, though closely connected to it.

Had Jesus left us with personal written instructions in the faith, it would have made the theory of *Sola Scriptura* as sole authority of the Church more palatable. Instead, I learned that both Scripture *and* Tradition are tools of the Holy Spirit; and these two living tools do not conflict. The Catholic Church does not teach that Sacred Tradition supersedes the written Word. The faith of the churches, founded in the first four centuries after Christ, were formed and nourished by the Sacred Tradition of truths

---

[18] The words catechism, catechize, and catechist are Latinizations for the Greek root katēkhízō (κατηχίζω) which means to "instruct orally." It is not unique to the Catholic Church, but a popular method of instruction used to teach a subject matter, typically in a Q&A format.

transmitted from mouth to ear. Prior to the Council of
Rome (382 A.D.), there had been no apostolic "table of
contents" delineating which books should be included
(canonized) or excluded in the compilation of the New
Testament. It was at this Catholic Council, under the direction of the Holy Spirit, that gave all of Christianity the
twenty-seven books of the New Testament we read today.

> *Baptists do not recognize any authoritative value regarding
> Tradition, but follow the idea, largely promulgated by John
> Calvin, of Sola Scriptura (Latin for "only Scripture") as the
> Sacred authority of the Church.*

The Lord's Supper (and the Real Presence of Christ)

Baptists loudly collide with the Catholic Church on the sig-
nificance of the Eucharist or Lord's Supper. Beginning
with Scripture, we read:

> While they were eating, Jesus took bread,
> said the blessing, broke it, and giving it to
> his disciples said, "Take and eat; this is my
> body." Then he took a cup, gave thanks,
> and gave it to them, saying, "Drink from it,
> all of you, for this is my blood of the

covenant, which will be shed on behalf of
many for the forgiveness of sins. (Matthew
26:26-28)

While they were eating, he took bread, said
the blessing, broke it, and gave it to them,
and said, "Take it; this is my body." Then he
took a cup, gave thanks, and gave it to them,
and they all drank from it. He said to them,
"This is my blood of the covenant, which
will be shed for many. (Mark 14:22-24)

When the hour came, he took his place at
table with the apostles. He said to them, "I
have eagerly desired to eat this Passover
with you before I suffer, for, I tell you, I
shall not eat it [again] until there is fulfill-
ment in the kingdom of God." Then he
took a cup, gave thanks, and said, "Take this
and share it among yourselves; for I tell you
[that] from this time on I shall not drink of
the fruit of the vine until the kingdom of
God comes." Then he took the bread, said
the blessing, broke it, and gave it to them,
saying, "This is my body, which will be

given for you; do this in memory of me."
And likewise the cup after they had eaten,
saying, "This cup is the new covenant in my
blood, which will be shed for you. (Luke
22:14-20)

Although the Gospel of John does not specifically mention the Last Supper event, he does write a discourse on the *Bread of Life*, in Chapter 6, where we find Jesus contending with unbelieving Jews over the Mosaic manna from heaven and asserting himself as the new manna from heaven.

So Jesus said to them, "Amen, amen, I say
to you, it was not Moses who gave the
bread from heaven; my Father gives you
the true bread from heaven. For the bread
of God is that which comes down from
heaven and gives life to the world." So
they said to him, "Sir, give us this bread
always." Jesus said to them, "I am the
bread of life; whoever comes to me will
never hunger, and whoever believes in me
will never thirst. (John 6:32-35)

Your ancestors ate the manna in the desert, but they died; this is the bread that comes down from heaven so that one may eat it and not die. I am the living bread that came down from heaven; whoever eats this bread will live forever; and the bread that I will give is my flesh for the life of the world." The Jews quarreled among themselves, saying, "How can this man give us [his] flesh to eat?" Jesus said to them, "Amen, amen, I say to you, unless you eat the flesh of the Son of Man and drink his blood, you do not have life within you. Whoever eats my flesh and drinks my blood has eternal life, and I will raise him on the last day. For my flesh is true food, and my blood is true drink. Whoever eats my flesh and drinks my blood remains in me and I in him. Just as the living Father sent me and I have life because of the Father, so also the one who feeds on me will have life because of me. (John 6:49-57)

In all four Gospels, Jesus is reported as saying, *eat my flesh / drink my blood*. God, who is not the author of confusion, instability or disorder (1 Cor.14:33), did not further clarify the meaning of these words. Even though the Jews were confused by the statement, and many of his disciples who were listening said - *This saying is hard; who can accept it?* - Jesus did not explain himself, but replied in verse 61, *Does this shock you?* I had to ask myself, "Would Jesus ever leave his followers to wonder if he was being literal or simply figurative?"

††††

During the first few hundred years of the Church, Christians were accused of seditious, even heinous acts, including infanticide and calling the Lord's Supper "cannibalism." They were myths, of course, perpetrated against the early Christians, in part through ignorance and in part from the disdain with which Greeks, Romans and Jews viewed Christianity.[19] More than a thousand years later,

---

[19] Celsus, an influential second century Greek Philosopher, railed against the early Christians in his work *The True Word* (ca. 175 A.D.), calling Christianity a religion of fools filled with the lowest of societies' classes.

the Church would again face ridicule regarding the Lord's Supper, only this time the accusers would be Christian.

During the Reformation, the rejection of the Catholic Eucharist would be used as a weapon against the Church's long-established teaching. Early Christianity, however, substantiates the Catholic position on the Real Presence of Christ in the consecrated bread and wine of the Eucharist. Below are examples of early Church defenders of the Catholic teaching:

Justin (ca. 110-165 A.D.)

One of the first apologists for Christianity, and guardian of the Catholic Sacrament of the Eucharist, was a man named Justin. He was born into a pagan family in the Roman province of Palestine, and not unlike myself, moved from one school of thought to another. On his journey, he discovered Christianity and became one of her greatest and most articulate apologists.

When pagans began to rail publicly against Christianity, Justin came to her defense. In writing to Antonius Pius (Roman Emperor from 138-161 A.D.) and the Roman Senate, Justin refuted inaccurate reports of Christian conduct and worship. In his *First Apology*, the portion addressing the Eucharist, he wrote:

We call this food Eucharist; and no one else is permitted to partake of it, except one who believes our teaching to be true and who has been washed in the washing which is for the remission of sins and for regeneration, and is thereby living as Christ enjoined. For not as common bread nor common drink do we receive these; but since Jesus Christ our Savior was made incarnate by the word of God and had both flesh and blood for our salvation, so to, as we have been taught, the food which has been made into the Eucharist by the Eucharistic prayer set down by Him, and by the change of which our blood and flesh is nourished, is both the flesh and the blood of that incarnated Jesus.

The Apostles, in the Memoirs, which they produced, which are called Gospels, have thus passed on that which was enjoined to them: that Jesus took bread, and having given thanks, said, 'Do this in remembrance of Me; this is My Body.' And in like manner, taking the cup, and having

given thanks, He said, 'This is My Blood.'
And He imparted this to them only.[20]

In other words, *Dear Emperor Pius*, if you were to personally attend our Eucharistic service, <u>you</u> would see us eat
and drink ordinary bread and wine, but it is <u>we</u> who believe
it to be divine flesh and blood which nourishes our soul.
His argument showed that cannibalism was a vitriolic
myth.

Justin was among the first public defenders of the faith
and practice of the early Church. He fortified the true
meaning of the Eucharist through homilies, letters, and
catechisms. Around 165 A.D., he and six companions were
beheaded by the Roman government, and he would forever be known to us as Justin the Martyr.

Ignatius of Antioch, Bishop of Antioch (ca. 50-107 A.D.)

Ignatius, who resided in what is now modern Syria, after
having been arrested by Roman officials, wrote seven letters addressed to seven different churches while enroute to

---

[20] Jurgens, W.A., trans. And ed. *The Faith of the Early Fathers, Vol. I.* (Collegeville: The Liturgical Press, 1970), p. 55.

his martyrdom in Rome. Among those letters, three referenced the Eucharist.

> To the Romans: "I desire the Bread of God, which is the Flesh of Jesus Christ, who was the seed of David, and for drink I desire His Blood, which is love incorruptible."

> To the Philadelphians: "Take care, then, to use one Eucharist, so that whatever you do, you do according to God: for there is one Flesh of our Lord Jesus Christ, and one cup in the union of His Blood; one altar, as there is one bishop with the presbytery and my fellow servants, the deacons."

> To the Smyrnaeans: "Take note of those who hold heterodox opinions... They abstain from the Eucharist and from prayer, because they do not confess that the Eucharist is the Flesh of our Savior Jesus Christ,

Flesh which suffered for our sins which the
Father, in His goodness, raised up again."[21]

Ignatius would defend the faith, including this Sacred Tradition grounded in Sacred Scripture, with his own life. Under Emperor Trajan, he was fed to the lions, ca. 108 A.D.

Irenaeus, Bishop of Lyons (ca. 140-202 A.D.)

Irenaeus, who resided in what is now modern France, the
author of a great apologetic work against the Gnostics entitled *Against Heresies*, wrote on the Eucharist:

> For as the bread from the earth, receiving
> the invocation of God, is no longer com-
> mon bread but the Eucharist, consisting of
> two elements, earthly and heavenly, so also
> our bodies, when they receive the Eucha-
> rist, are no longer corruptible but have the
> hope of resurrection into eternity.[22]

[21] Jurgens, W.A., trans. And ed. *The Faith of the Early Fa-thers, Vol. I.* (Collegeville: The Liturgical Press, 1970), pp. 17-25.
[22] Jurgens, W.A., trans. And ed. *The Faith of the Early Fa-thers, Vol. I.* (Collegeville: The Liturgical Press, 1970), p. 95.

Clement, Bishop of Alexandria (ca. 150- 211 A.D.)

Clement, who resided in what is now modern Egypt, wrote a work intitled *Exhortation to the Greeks*, wherein he stated:

> The Blood of the Lord, indeed, is twofold. There is His corporeal Blood, by which we are redeemed from corruption; and His spiritual Blood, that with which we are anointed. That is to say, to drink the Blood of Jesus is to share in His immortality. Those who partake of it in faith are sanctified in body and in soul.
>
> ... mystically united to the Spirit and to the Word.[23]

Ephraim, Deacon of the Syrian Church (ca. 306-373 A.D.)

In his *Homilies*, Ephraim wrote:

---

[23] Jurgens, W.A., trans. And ed. *The Faith of the Early Fathers, Vol. I.* (Collegeville: The Liturgical Press, 1970), p. 179.

Take, eat, entertaining no doubt of faith,
because this is My Body, and whoever eats
it in belief eats in it Fire and Spirit. For if
any doubter eat of it, for him it will be only
bread.[24]

From Alexandria to Antioch, and Lyons to Rome, history revealed that the Catholic Church believed and professed the Real Presence of Christ in the consecrated bread and wine of the Eucharist.

†††

Theological disputes surrounding the bread and wine rose to prominence during the Reformation era; however, the dispute was nothing new to the Catholic Church. Long before the Reformation, there were factions who denied the Real Presence of Christ in the consecrated bread and wine. For example, the 10th Century Bogomils and 12th Century Cathars (also called Albigensians), considered by some as proto-Protestants and included in the Baptist Succession-ist Theory, taught that the Eucharist was strictly symbolic.

---

[24] Jurgens, W.A., trans. And ed. *The Faith of the Early Fathers, Vol. I.* (Collegeville: The Liturgical Press, 1970), pp. 311.

And while 16th century Reformers may have been encouraged by this historical aspect, these neo-Gnostic groups espoused other heretical beliefs, such as the dualism of God. To cherry-pick one historical tenet from an otherwise heretical group of separatists is questionable support for the teaching of symbolism and an invalid reason to schism from traditional Church teaching. What I have found today is that there are Christians who are unwilling to accept the words of Jesus at face value. And as a former fundamentalist Baptist I find this ironic because biblical literalism is highly praised in fundamental circles, and, yet, on this particular point, Jesus' own words are not considered accurate.

Symbolism, parables, and mysteries are all part of Christian teaching, and each serves a distinct purpose. The Last Supper was not symbolic, or parabolic, but Jesus instituting something otherworldly—a mystery. As such, I had to ask myself, despite the strangeness of his teaching, could I deny him a literal meaning? The answer was no, for to deny him a literal meaning was to place greater trust in my human wisdom than God's wisdom. And from the earliest

days of Christianity, Tradition has taken Jesus at his institutional word.

Reflecting on the Catholic Church's continuum of care
for the historical meaning of the Eucharist, below is the
definition from the *Catechism of the Catholic Church*
(1358):

> We must therefore consider the Eucharist
> as: thanksgiving and praise to the Father;
> the sacrificial memorial of Christ and his
> body; the presence of Christ by the power
> of his word and of his Spirit.

---

*Baptist believe that the Lord's Supper is a symbolic memo-
rial, while Lutherans have their own interpretation of the
real presence called "consubstantiation." All, however, differ
from the "real presence of Christ," theologically referred to
as "transubstantiation;" a 12th century term that was applied to Church's already traditional understanding.*

Re-sacrificing Christ at the Mass

Another misunderstood teaching of the Church, directly
linked with the Eucharist, is that Christ is *re-sacrificed*
again at every Mass. The idea is so horrific it does not seem

right to address it, but it is still perceived as such by many non-Catholic Christians today. For that reason alone, I have included it here.

The English word "mass," (German *messa*, French *masse*) is used in conjunction with the Catholic Church and was derived from the 6-7th-century Latin phrase *Ite missa est* ("Go, it is dismissed") spoken at the conclusion of the worship service. *Ite missa est* followed the Eucharistic Celebration, the last, but central part of the service. "Mass" became the common term used by Catholics, shorthand if you will, for the entire act of worship, although technically speaking the "Mass" is the "Eucharistic Celebration." (I admit that navigating Catholic terminology is a lesson in itself, but knowing what words mean clarifies understanding.)

The Catholic act of worship is manifested in the liturgy, or what most Protestants call the service or order of worship. The liturgy includes music (hymns), prayers, readings from Scripture (both Old and New Testaments), readings from the Gospels, a homily, then concludes with the Eucharist and dismissal.

In the *Catechism of the Catholic Church*, it states:

> (1356) If from the beginning Christians have celebrated the eucharist and in a form

whose substance has not changed despite
the great diversity of times and liturgies, it
is because we know ourselves to be bound
by the command the Lord gave on the eve
of his Passion: "Do this in remembrance of
me."

(1357) We carry out this command of the
Lord by celebrating *the memorial of his sacrifice*. In so doing, *we offer to the Father*
what he has himself given us: the gifts of his
creation, bread and wine which, by the
power of the Holy Spirit and the words of
Christ, have become the body and blood of
Christ. Christ is thus really and mysteri-
ously made *present*.

The Catholic Church does not re-sacrifice Jesus in the
Mass but teaches that the sacrifice of the Lamb of God on
the Cross was a one-time-and-for-all historical event. That
King Jesus Christ is seated at the right hand of the Father
today is undoubted. To understand, as much as humanly
possible, the Eucharist as a living sacrifice, we can look at
it from the perspective of created time.

Human beings are the only lifeform on earth who live by the second hand of a clock. We are driven by precision. This creation called "time" has an invisible power over us, as we are often constrained by time, waste time, and even include time in contractual agreements (e.g., the clause "time is of the essence.") But God, infinite and eternal, does not view time from our perspective.

My father, who was a great doodler, used to enjoy drawing three-dimensional objects and quirky stuff like a railroad track vanishing into the horizon. He told me that perspective is important because we often think we see what is untrue. On paper, the train tracks look like they come to a point and disappear, but in reality, they don't. Likewise, our perspective of time differs from God's, and his is the true vantage point.

God reveals a glimpse of his relationship to created time when he declares to Moses, "I am that I am," in Exodus 3:14. God is *I AM*, always in the present tense. From his eternal "present" perspective, he is not subject to created time. In both Psalms 90:4 and II Peter 3:8, we read that for God, a day is like a thousand years and a thousand years like a day. God just does not see time as we do.

The sacrificial death, burial, and resurrection of Jesus Christ unfolded in created time and space. For Christians today, they were historical events, yet to God, all created things, including time, are *continually before his eyes.* As such, the sacrifice of Jesus Christ is ever-present to God. And the Eucharist, the thanksgiving celebrated by the Catholic Church, re-enacts *a memorial for our benefit of the ever-present sacrifice of Jesus Christ.* The Lord's Supper is a sacrament in which <u>we</u> remember the once-for-all sacrifice of the Lamb of God.

Baptism

At the age of six, I realized that I did not have Jesus in my heart. I recall clearly after a Sunday service, and while riding home in the car, I went roundabout asking if each occupant, mother, father and brother, if each were "saved." For each question the answer was met with a "yes." At that point, I pronounced "Then, I am saved too!" and all three unanimously replied "No!" I pouted all the way home.

That very evening my father, who was still a student in seminary, was preaching, and at the end of the service I told my mother that I wanted to go forward and accept Jesus. She said, "go on then," and I walked that long aisle down to my father. We prayed, and I asked Jesus into my heart. My mother told me years later that it was the first time in a service that I had not "doodled" on paper or put my head in her lap; I had actually listened to the message. Six months later, I was baptized.

There is a great deal of debate surrounding Baptism in general and infant Baptism in specific that I wanted to understand. The first thing I did was dig into scripture, and then I looked at the tradition of the early Church (Catholic), versus the Baptist understanding of Baptism. Were they as diametrically opposed as I had been raised to believe? Was one practiced correctly, while the other not? These were my questions. And once again, I was dismayed that there was no consensus among Christians.

What is Baptism?

The word baptize comes from the Greek, *baptizó* (βαπτίζω), and is a rite of cleansing or washing. It was first applied in the New Testament by John the Baptist, and second, as a rite of salvation.

Under John the Baptist, the last prophet of the Old Covenant, the Hebrew people were called to ceremonially *wash* away their *repented* sin. Matt. 3:11, "I baptize you with water for repentance." Repentance and washing went hand-in-hand with John's message. It was not a "saving" Baptism, but a call for Hebrews to change their hardened hearts "for the kingdom of heaven is near."

After John the Baptist, and the Resurrection of Jesus, the practice of Baptism took on a similar, yet different aspect. No longer a call only to Hebrews for repentance, baptism became available to all regardless of ethnicity. It was the washing away of original sin (the spiritual rebirth of the person) and the presentation of a person as a new creature in Christ. Both Catholics and Baptists practice one Baptism "in the name of the Father, the Son, and the Holy Spirit," and that it is a command (Matthew 28:19). Both understand that it publicly represents the death, burial, and resurrection of Jesus Christ. Both Catholics and Baptists pronounce, "I baptize you, (person's name), in the name of the Father, and of the Son, and of the Holy Spirit." Baptists, who use strictly immersion, also add during the ceremony, "Buried in the likeness of his death, raised in the likeness of his resurrection."

The issue between Catholics and Baptist, that I discovered, rests in two areas: the inherent meaning of Baptism, and the order of Baptism in conjunction with repentance.

The Meaning of Baptism

For Baptists, Baptism is a public ceremony in which a person who has already converted to Christianity follows in obedience to the faith by Baptism. In Baptism, the new believer is identified with the risen Christ, thus fulfilling the command in Matthew's gospel.

For Catholics, Baptism is more than a symbol or act of obedience: it confirms a sacrament of grace and washes away original sin.

The Order of Baptism and Repentance

Baptists adhere strictly to "believer's baptism," which means that Baptism comes *after* a person has believed and repented. Because it requires belief and repentance first, infants are not baptized. There is no minimum age, but most consider 7+ years to be an "age of accountability" (when a child knows right from wrong). While Baptists do not Baptize infants, parents often "dedicate" their newborns in a public ceremony, appropriately called, a "baby dedication." The parents, with the help of their church, promise to raise their child in Christ.

Catholics, like Baptists, also practice "believers baptism" as well as infant baptism. Kenneth Baker sums this up nicely when he states:

> The normal person to receive baptism is the adult who has heard the gospel and has come to believe that Jesus is the Lord. The

basic dispositions necessary to receive Christian baptism fruitfully are faith and sorrow for one's sins. St. Peter concluded his first sermon on the Pentecost with the admonition that his hearers should believe in the Good News, "repent" and "be baptized in the name of Jesus Christ for the forgiveness of your sins." (Acts 2:38)

All are reminded that the Baptism of infants is the exception rather than the rule in the history of the Church. The infant has no personal sins, (only original sin) for which to repent; but he or she must have faith in some way. Catholic teaching stresses that the faith of the Church supplies for the child until it is able to make an act of faith on its own.[25]

In the Catholic Church, baptism is seen as the washing away of *original* sin—the sin all humans are born with. As such, Catholic's practice "infant baptism" in the presence of their parents (and god-parents) as a washing away of

---

[25] Fundamentals of Catholicism, Vol. 1; Kenneth Baker, S.J. (Ignatius press: NY, 1982), p. 112.

original sin and their (parents and god-parents) dedication to raise the child in the Church. Actual repentance of personal sin and conversion come when a child has attained a certain age and understanding.

Baptists more often than not do not recognize a Catholic Baptism as "valid" and require rebaptism, in large part because Baptists do not view the Catholic Church as part of the "true" Church. Catholicism, on the other hand, recognizes most forms of Protestant Baptism[26] and will not rebaptize. In my case, I presented my baptismal certificate from a Baptist Church, and my baptism was considered valid.

Does Baptism alone "save" a person?

For Baptists, a person may be reconciled to God (saved) with repentance and true conversion; baptism is encouraged, but not necessary for salvation. It is a public and symbolic gesture of an already converted person.

---

[26] The Catholic Church does <u>not</u> recognize the Baptism of many so-called churches or religious movements, for example, Jehovah's Witnesses, Latter Day Saints (Mormons), and Oneness Pentecostals.

For Catholics, Baptism is more than a symbol, but a sacrament of grace that washes away original sin and a necessary component of salvation (John 3:1-7).

> Now there was a man of the Pharisees, named Nicodemus, a ruler of the Jews; this man came to Jesus by night and said to Him, "Rabbi, we know that You have come from God as a teacher; for no one can do these signs that You do unless God is with him." Jesus answered and said to him, "Truly, truly, I say to you, unless one is born again he cannot see the kingdom of God." Nicodemus said to Him, "How can a man be born when he is old? He cannot enter a second time into his mother's womb and be born, can he?" Jesus answered, **"Truly, truly, I say to you, unless one is born of water and the Spirit he cannot enter into the kingdom of God.** "That which is born of the flesh is flesh, and that which is born of the Spirit is spirit. "Do not be amazed that I said to you, 'You must be born again.'

For the adult, it comes after conversion (faith and repentance). For the infant, Baptism is the first step *toward* conversion (faith and repentance).

My final thoughts on this is that for myself, it does not matter. I was baptized according to Sacred Scripture and that was sufficient for my conversion. However, that Baptism has become such a point of contention among Christians is more a human problem than a God problem. Whether Baptism comes first then conversion or conversion first then Baptism is of no consequence to me. All I know is that Jesus wants BOTH, and in the end, God will judge.

CHAPTER TWELVE

What about the *Other* Stuff?

I can hear my Baptist brethren already; *but what about all the other stuff?* By "other stuff" they (and most Protestants) mean the creeds, as well as post-Nicene Catholic teaching on indulgences; purgatory, prayers for the dead, the Immaculate Conception of Mary, *Ex Cathedra*, Rite of Reconciliation (confession), and more. My approach to answer these items, for myself, was both two-fold and simultaneous. First, I did my homework, looking into the what and why of each teaching. Second, I practiced my faith in the guiding direction of the Holy Spirit over the Church as a unified Body of Christ.

By studying the various teachings, I was able to understand all of them. Simple enough, yet it also meant that though I understood I may not have liked what I learned, and this is where the consumer mentality often meddles where it ought not because "liking" a teaching should not be a factor in belief and obedience. For me to sit in judgment of what was clearly understood because I simply did not like the teaching is a subjective (and prideful) response to an objective truth. The teachings of the Church, even the basics of all Christian tenets, are God revealed truths that are not to be viewed as relative, but absolute. That is not something most westerners, especially Americans, like to hear, and that was my case for many years early on.

Even today, and speaking quite frankly, I don't *like* a lot of what Scripture has to say on many subjects. Revealed truths, however, such as Sacred Scripture, are not subject to personal interpretations, particularly when one is looking for a "loop-hole" such as justifying pre-marital or same-sex marriage between Christians. The world may do as it likes, and frequently does, but our calling is not of this world. Thomas Jefferson, who was not a Christian, had no inkling of revelation when he carved out whole portions of the New Testament he did not like.

When I was welcomed into full communion with the Roman Catholic Church, I and my fellow RCIA candidates stated in unison, "I believe and profess all that the Holy Catholic Church believes, teaches and proclaims to be revealed by God." It was a statement that I could make without reservation, not because I blindly believed, or that I "liked" everything the Church teaches, but because I realized that the authority to teach on faith and morals is bestowed upon the Church and not upon individuals.

At a time when people have an opinion on everything, *and* think that they are correct, the idea of removing myself from the equation of what the Church should and should not teach may seem sheep-like; and it is, sort of. It is certainly undemocratic, much like the company I worked for.

As an executive in commercial real estate and development, my line of work was guided, in part, by what we called "deal breakers." Contractual negotiations were made within the company's corporate guidelines of what would, and would not, be acceptable terms to conclude a transaction. Any proposed term that would compromise a core value was called a deal breaker and essentially stopped the negotiation before it reached a first draft. Other than that, any item that fell outside the core criteria would be considered by the executive committee that was headed by our company president. Analogous to the Church, my company had a hierarchy of authority and a guideline everyone was expected to follow.

In the Church, as with my company, I am a part, but not the authoritative whole. The earliest guideline, provided by the Church, was the Nicene Creed, the ecumenical summary of core Christian beliefs. Since then, teach-

ings on faith and morals that fall outside the Creed, and
that do not conflict with Scripture, are the responsibility of
the Catholic Church to address. I may espouse an opinion,
but that does not translate into authority. Now, it may
sound like I am throwing the Pope, the 21 Councils, and
the Magisterium under a bus (God forbid), but I recognized that I, as a lay person, am not responsible for official
Church teachings. No more than an administrative assis-
tant is responsible for the decision of an executive committee.

†††

As a child, I often did not understand what I was taught,
but I trusted my parents. And now, as an adult Catholic, I
understand a good deal, but more importantly, I accept it
because I trust the Holy Spirit to faultlessly direct the
Church. The willingness to acquiesce on the "other stuff"
and defer to the Church's teaching authority did not mean
checking my mind at the door, but willfully tossing my
pride out the window.

Pride, whether it be from self-determination or self-
satisfaction, is an individual's sin against God. God is Love,
but he also hates, and he hates pride and haughtiness,

referenced in both the Old and New Testaments (Prov. 8:13, Prov. 16:18, Isa. 10:33, Luke 18:11, I Cor. 8:1, Jas. 4:6, and I Peter 5:5). Now, the Catholic Church is made up of individuals, indeed people who sin, but as individuals they are neither *the* Church, nor independent of the Church. The Church is not, and never has been, a democratic institution. Vested by Christ, she consists of a hierarchy of leadership, which functions under the guidance of the Holy Spirit. This human and divine structure ensures the fidelity of the faith as it is transmitted throughout the ages.

When it comes to the official teachings of the Church, the responsibility of the laity, that's me, is to trust God as he divinely directs his one, holy, catholic, and apostolic church. This direction was clearly seen in the 4th century when Church leadership had to combat the Arian heresy. A lay person, or even a rebellious priest like Arius, may have a personal opinion about a teaching, but the authority for discernment in truth and error, in faith and morals, is firmly planted with the Church.

CHAPTER THIRTEEN

Final Thoughts

The chapters above are a sample of what an inquiring mind may discover, if only they seek. This book was never meant to be an apologetic, but a conversion story—complex though it was.

During decades of doubt and confusion, I discovered that no other system of belief could adequately answer my quest for meaning in life, except Christianity. And I learned that the Catholic Church traces its origin and authority directly to the Apostles. During the infancy of the faith, the Catholic Church through ecumenical councils gave us the Nicene Creed, provided a compilation of gospels and letters called the New Testament, and defended the integrity of the faith against enemies both without and within. God truly blessed her with dedicated and gifted early fathers who took on the momentous task of refuting error. Guided by no less than the Holy Spirit, the Church is a divine and human structure, the Body and Bride of Christ who shed his blood for her.

Since the 16th century, a time of both political and religious upheaval, the Catholic Church has strived to remain faithful to her now 2,000-year-old apostolic roots. Her leaders understand the grave importance of the unity of the faith enshrined in the one, holy, and apostolic Church of the Nicene Creed. The Reformation, which produced the greatest schism within the Body of Christ since the East/West schism of 1054 A.D., has continued to inspire division and even normalize the concept. It is most unfortunate that for over 500 years Christianity has been disheveled, fraught with bickering, and confusing to both Christians and those in need of salvation.

Although I am personally saddened by the historical schisms that have resulted in a state of Christian disunity, that does not mean that either party, Protestant or Catholic, is exclusively to blame. As a student of Church history, and attempting to be as objective as humanly possible, I believe that early Reformers, whom we must remember were Roman Catholic (Luther had been a Monk), had the best of intentions in trying to internally correct what they considered to be error, right or wrong, and that the Catholic Church was slow to respond.[27] At the same time,

---

[27] As a Catholic Monk, it was in 1517 that Martin Luther posted his 95 Theses on the door of the Wittenberg Church, but it was not until 1545 at the Council of Trent that the Catholic

however, I can see that those intentions opened a pandora's box of ambiguity, dissent, and ultimately division from the historic Body of Christ.

What should have, and could have, been reformed from within the Church became a very public disagreement on everything from Church structure to Scriptural interpretation. And the growing pool of first, then second-generation Reformers only served to fracture the Church further as Christ was now being offered a Bride with multiple bodies. There is but one Head and one Body, and, as such, someone had to be right and someone had to be wrong and above all, schism was not the answer.

One of my favorite authors is G.K. Chesterton (1874-1936). In his book *Heretics*, he frequently states that so-and-so believes this or that, "but he is wrong." I enjoy Chesterton's frankness, yet I also understand that no one likes to admit when they are wrong; because to admit that

---

Church mounted her own Catholic Revival, sometimes referred to as the Catholic Reformation, to address concerns raised by some Catholics. By the time the council met at Trent, however, Protestors from Switzerland to England had already begun to flourish with no small help from anti-Papal princes who protected Reformers often for their own political gain. In this regard, the break from Rome was as much politically motivated as it was theologically.

is to dent one's pride. But pride should never accompany belief.

Pride asserts the supremacy of self and is perhaps the most unacceptable behavior for a follower of Christ. Yet you may ask me, "What if I say that I am humbly convinced that infant baptism is error?" My Chestertonian reply would be, "You are still wrong." A personal conviction or opinion, whether grounded in humility or pride, or sanctioned by many or few, is invalid when contrary to historic Catholic Church teaching. At this point, an astute reader will respond, "Well, Chesterton was a Catholic," but that bears no weight in this argument, for though Chesterton pointed out that no two opposing answers can be simultaneously true, his is not a Catholic thought. Chesterton was merely reiterating a construct of logic—the Law of Non-Contradiction. And this law is pretty straightforward. If I say my dog is a Shih Tsu and in my next breath state that she is not a Shih Tsu, I have contradicted myself; only one statement can be valid if it is to be realistic. And to be realistic is to understand that there is certain truth because God is reality.

Because God is reality, or what the Evangelical theologian and philosopher Francis Schaeffer referred to as "true truth," God cannot be the author of confusion, for his truths are absolute. Therefore, if one church states, "Baptism is the sacrament of regeneration," and another church says "Baptism is <u>not</u> a sacrament of regeneration," one of them is incorrect, and this is exactly the state of contradiction in which Christianity exists today.

†††

After my initial return to Christianity, and my subsequent search for a church, I was deeply troubled by the many conflicting doctrines. Even before I read Chesterton, or was reminded of the law of non-contradiction from my college days, I knew that contrary beliefs had no place in the Church. Through diligent prayer and by studying the Scriptures and Early Church History, I was able to see that the Catholic Church is the legitimate continuation of the New Testament Church and appreciate that nothing about the development of Catholic teaching is haphazard. In fact, it can take months or even years to coalesce a decision on an issue of faith and morals, yet once the decision has been made, the Church clarifies her teaching with extraordinary detail. This is exemplified in the documents of Vatican II, which took years to complete and are available to anyone in book form.

It is difficult for individuals, especially Americans, to accept that their "vote" does not count in the formation of doctrinal teachings; the primacy of the individual is entrenched in our society. And though Jesus loves us individually, when it comes to authoritative decision-making that impacts the whole Body of Christ, Jesus bestowed that upon the Church and not the individual.

†††

Since joining the Catholic Church, I have entered into a human family that traces back two millennia. The people who make up that family, including myself, are imperfect, yet they are still the family of God. It is a family that lives today, both on earth and in heaven, that praises God through her rich, historic liturgy that incorporates hymns and prayers, Scripture readings and homilies, and concludes with holy thanksgiving in the Eucharist. She strives for unity of mind and spirit, and she is the historic defender of the New Testament Church, the Body and Bride of Christ. Her continuum of care toward the fidelity of the faith is reflected throughout history. The Catholic Church has become my home, my place of worship, and my rest beside still waters. Not only have I learned to appreciate and respect her, but I have begun to love her as well.

†††

My convoluted journey, from Fundamentalist Baptist to Roman Catholic by way of agnosticism, was often tiresome and painful. It required perseverance to keep searching for the truth I knew was out there. And though I ultimately found the truth, in returning to Christianity fifteen years ago, the real journey had only just begun. What I had initially gained when I returned to God was a sure foundation, but I did not stop there.

Our life is continually under construction as we work toward the goal of accomplishing what God has planned for us. The Apostle Paul likened his life to a race, and considered himself to be constantly running toward the finish line. He fully understood that Christianity is not a spectator sport, but a life of action.

That's the end of my story, at least for you the reader. One last thing before I go, let me say that wherever you may be in your spiritual journey, please understand two important things. First, if you seek, you will find. Second, there is no such thing as a stupid question.

APPENDIX I

First Council of Nicaea (325)	First Council of Constantinople (381)
We believe in one God, the Father Almighty, Maker of all things visible and invisible.	We believe in one God, the Father Almighty, Maker of heaven and earth, and of all things visible and invisible.
And in one Lord Jesus Christ, the Son of God, begotten of the Father [the only-begotten; that is, of the essence of the Father, God of God], Light of Light, very God of very God, begotten, not made, being of one substance with the Father;	And in one Lord Jesus Christ, the only-begotten Son of God, begotten of the Father before all worlds, Light of Light, very God of very God, begotten, not made, being of one substance with the Father;
by whom all things were made [both in heaven and on earth];	by whom all things were made;
who for us men, and for our salvation, came down and was incarnate and was made man;	who for us men, and for our salvation, came down from heaven, and was incarnate by the Holy Spirit of the Virgin Mary, and was made man;
he suffered, and the third day he rose again, ascended into heaven;	he was crucified for us under Pontius Pilate, and suffered, and was buried, and the third day he rose again, according to the Scriptures, and ascended into

	heaven, and sits on the right hand of the Father;
from thence he shall come to judge the quick and the dead.	from thence he shall come again, with glory, to judge the quick and the dead;
	whose kingdom shall have no end.
And in the Holy Spirit.	And in the Holy Spirit, the Lord and Giver of life, who proceeds from the Father, who with the Father and the Son together is worshiped and glorified, who spoke by the prophets. In one holy catholic and apostolic Church; we acknowledge one baptism for the remission of sins; we look for the resurrection of the dead, and the life of the world to come. Amen.
[But those who say: 'There was a time when he was not;' and 'He was not before he was made;' and 'He was made out of nothing,' or 'He is of another substance' or 'essence,' or 'The Son of God is created,' or 'changeable,' or 'alterable' — they are condemned by the holy catholic and apostolic Church.]	

APPENDIX II

100	200	300	400	500	600	700	800	900	1000
IRREGULAR CHURCHES	CHURCH GOVERNMENT CHANGED		CHURCH AND STATE UNITED	LEO II POPERY OFICIALLY ESTABLISHED				DIVISION	INFANT COMMUNION
		(HIERARCHY)				(CATHOLIC)		(869)	GREE
JESUS ORGANIZES HIS CHURCH MARK 3:16-18	BAPTISMAL REGENERATION	CONSTANTINE 313	MARIOLOTRY				SAINT AND IMAGE WORSHIP 787		ROMAN
		INFANT BAPTISM	PERSECUTION ACT 303	INFANT BAPTISM ESTABLISHED BY LAW		PURGATORY			
		NON FELLOWSHIP DECLARED 251			INDULGENCES				
			TOLERATION ACT 311					DARK	AGE

100	200	300	400	500	600	700	800	900	1000
	MONTANISTS NOVATIONS	PURITANS	PATERINS CATHARI			PAULICIAN			
CHRISTIANS		A N A			B A P T I S T S				
	PATERINS	D O N	A T I S T S						F
	ITALY WALES		SPAIN FRANCE		W A L E S				IT
					ARMENIA	ITALY ENGLAND	ARMENIA BULGARIA		
ENGLAND		A F R I C A							

| 100 | 200 | 300 | 400 | 500 | 600 | 700 | 800 | 900 | 1000 |

BLOOD By DR. J. M. CARROLL

1100	1200	1300	1400	1500	1600	1700	1800	1900	2000

C A T H O L I C

K

TRENT 1483-1546 LUTHER

1123 CELIBACY

WYCLIFF 1330-1384

SAVONAROLA 1452-1498

(LUTHERAN)

1509-1564—CALVIN 1564—CUMBERLAND 1810

PETROBR-USIANS & ARNOLDISTS 1139

DEPOSED FREDERICK

TRANSUB-STANTIATION

(PRESBYTERIAN)

1541

1648 WESTPHALIA

1812 (DISCIPLES)

AURICULAR CONFESSION 1215

HUSS 1373-1415

1555 AUGS-BURG

(CONGREGATIONALIST) 1602

INQUISITION 1231

C A T H O L I C

ZWINGLI 1484-1531

CHURCH (OF ENGLAND)

1229 BIBLE FORBIDDEN

1531

(METHODIST)

1785

S

B A P (BAPTISTS)

BUNYAN 1628-1688

A B P.

ARNOLDISTS

ALBIGENSES

W A L D E N S E S

(CATA) (BAPTIST)

FRANCE HENRICIANS

A M E R I C A

G E R M A N Y

GERMANY

RUSSIA

ITALY

POLAND

CUBA

ENGLAND WALES

ALPS

FRANCE

SELECTED BIBLIOGRAPHY

Baker, Kenneth, SJ. *Fundamentals of Catholicism, Vol. I.* San Francisco: Ignatius Press, 1995.

Bellitto, Christopher M. *The General Councils: a history of the twenty-one Church Councils from Nicaea to Vatican II.* Mahwah: Paulist Press, 2002.

Benedict XVI. *Church Fathers: From Clement of Rome to Augustine.* San Francisco: Ignatius Press, 2008.

Catechism of the Catholic Church. 2nd ed. New York, NY: Doubleday, 1995.

Hahn, Scott. *The Creed: Professing the Faith Through the Ages.* Steubenville: Emmaus Road Publishing, 2016

Jurgens, W.A., ed. *The Faith of the Early Fathers, Vol. I.* Collegeville: The Liturgical Press, 1970.

Jurgens, W.A., ed. *The Faith of the Early Fathers, Vol. II & IIII.* Collegeville: The Liturgical Press, 1979.

Vidmar, John, OP. *The Catholic Church through the Ages: a history.* Mahwah: Paulist Press, 2016.

Made in the USA
Monee, IL
04 March 2023